# This Stops Today

# This Stops Today

## Eric Garner's Mother Seeks Justice after Losing Her Son

Gwen Carr
with Dave Smitherman

ROWMAN & LITTLEFIELD
Lanham • Boulder • New York • London

Published by Rowman & Littlefield
An imprint of The Rowman & Littlefield Publishing Group, Inc.
4501 Forbes Boulevard, Suite 200, Lanham, Maryland 20706
www.rowman.com

Unit A, Whitacre Mews, 26-34 Stannary Street, London SE11 4AB

Distributed by NATIONAL BOOK NETWORK

British Library Cataloguing in Publication Information Available

**Library of Congress Cataloging-in-Publication Data**
Names: Carr, Gwen, author. | Smitherman, Dave, co-author.
Title: This stops today : Eric Garner's mother seeks justice after losing her son /
    Gwen Carr with Dave Smitherman.
Description: Lanham : Rowman & Littlefield Publishing Group, Inc., [2018] |
    Includes bibliographical references and index.
Identifiers: LCCN 2018011674 (print) | LCCN 2018033576 (ebook) |
    ISBN 9781538109816 (electronic) | ISBN 9781538109809 (cloth : alk. paper)
Subjects: LCSH: Carr, Gwen. | Mothers—New York (State)—New York—
    Biography. | Police brutality—New York (State)—New York. | Police misconduct—
    New York (State)—New York. | Social justice—New York (State)—New York.
Classification: LCC HQ759 (ebook) | LCC HQ759 .C289 2018 (print) |
    DDC 306.874/3—dc23
LC record available at https://lccn.loc.gov/2018011674

Printed in the United States of America

Every time you see me, you want to harass me, you want to stop me. I'm so sick of it. I'm minding my business, officer. I'm minding my business. Please just leave me alone. I told you the last time, please just leave me alone. I did not do anything. . . . Please, please don't touch me. Do not touch me. . . . I can't breathe!

—Eric Garner

*In Memory of Erica Garner*

Erica, you are my son's first child, my first grandchild. I just can't come to grips with you being gone so soon. It seems you were here but a day, and now you've gone away. But your fight for your dad will live on in me, and so will my love for you and yours.

Mrs. Carr's incredible strength in the face of tragedy is monumental and awe inspiring. Though there are dark days, she continues to fight for the rights of victims everywhere. She was thrust into action because she had to; she did it for Eric. The fight for justice continues.

—Viola Davis and Julius Tennon,
coproducers of the TV docuseries *Two Sides*

# Contents

# Foreword

## Hillary Rodham Clinton

THE WRITER ELIZABETH STONE SAYS THAT having a child is forever deciding to have your heart go walking around outside your body. Those words were echoing in my mind the day I first met Gwen Carr and the other Mothers of the Movement. Over iced tea at the Sweet Maple Cafe on Chicago's West Side, I listened to the stories of these brokenhearted mothers. Despite living through every parent's worst nightmare, they radiated strength and quiet, fierce dignity. Their stories, and their strength, have stayed with me ever since. So has Gwen's declaration that she intended to turn her sorrow into a strategy, and her mourning into a movement. By channeling her private pain into public activism, and sharing her truth in the pages of this book, that's exactly what she has done.

It's easy to feel overwhelmed by all that's happening in our country, especially now—to read one heartbreaking headline after another and start to think, *There's nothing I can do, and it hurts too much to even try*. But we cannot grow weary of doing good. Just think of Gwen's resolve, her resilience, and her refusal to give up. She has endured some of the most painful circumstances imaginable—the excruciating loss of her firstborn, attempts to silence her voice, inaction from her own government, even attacks in the media. Yet, far from growing weary, she is doing everything she can to make our country a better place. As Gwen writes of her journey from quiet grandmother to unlikely activist, "I didn't know if I could make a real difference, but I did know that I could try." And so can we all.

From the title to the final page, Gwen's book is a powerful call to action for our country. It's also a deeply personal story that any parent can relate to—the story of a proud and loving mother determined to fight for her son. It can be a daunting challenge to pour your heart onto the page, to write candidly and courageously about things you may never even have spoken out loud. But with her trademark eloquence, Gwen bravely shines a light on her own doubts, her struggles, and her quest to push through her "limits and pain as a woman in her golden years who would rather be at home in her recliner." Not only that, but she also summons the generosity to share her son Eric with the world: "He was much more than just a Black man in a viral video. He was a caring, compassionate man who had love as wide as the ocean." Knowing Gwen is a gift, and so is reading this book.

I am grateful every day to Gwen for her friendship, and for her willingness to share her ideas and perspective with me with the same honesty and eloquence that radiates from these pages. These are complicated issues. But, as Gwen points out, "It's our responsibility to figure out what each of us can do to contribute." In our current political climate, reading and sharing books like Gwen's, and adding our voices to hers, is even more vital. And while progress is still too slow, when the opportunity arises to move forward and create real change, the policy principles Gwen has laid out in this book are a fantastic place to start.

In the meantime, each of us owes it to Gwen and the Mothers of the Movement to ask what we can do in our own lives—to follow Gwen's lead and refuse to grow complacent. At a minimum, we can start by facing hard truths, confronting our own implicit biases, and finding the courage to speak out. And we can try harder to walk in one another's shoes. That means police officers and all of us doing everything we can to understand the effects of systemic racism that young Black and Latino men and women face every day, and how they are made to feel like their lives are disposable. It also means imagining what it's like to be a police officer, kissing his or her kids and spouse goodbye every day and heading off to do a dangerous but necessary job. That kind of radical empathy isn't easy to come by in a time when divisions in our country run as deep as they do today. But I am convinced that it's what we need, now more than ever before.

The stories of the Mothers, and others who have lost loved ones to gun violence and police incidents, deserve to be told and heard. As Gwen writes, "Our children were people with hopes and dreams just like anyone else, and . . . they [deserve] to be remembered for more than just their violent ending." We have got to keep saying their names: Eric Garner, Sandra Bland, Michael Brown, Jordan Davis, Dontre Hamilton, Blair Holt, Trayvon Martin, Tamir Rice, Hadiya Pendleton—the list goes on. This cannot be seen as a political issue; it can and must be seen as an issue of fundamental justice and basic human decency. We should insist on nothing less from politicians, candidates, and anyone hoping to lead. The killing and mistreatment of young Black men and women has been the reality of life in America for too long. But we can't accept it as our inevitable future. Let's take Gwen's words to heart and ensure that this stops today.

# Chapter 1

─────────○─────────

# South Brooklyn

Angels in heaven, hear my plea. Take care of my baby, just for me.
—Unknown

ON JULY 17, 2014, I WAS working my job as a train operator for the New York Metropolitan Transit Authority (MTA). I had just driven to Queens and was taking a break when my phone started blowing up. Calls, messages—they just kept coming. I was underground and totally unaware of the happenings in the bustling city above. I could tell from the sheer volume of messages that something was wrong, but I was working and couldn't get the whole story. Something about my son, Eric. I called my husband, Ben, and said, "I just heard that something happened to Eric. I'm not sure what's going on. Can you meet me at Stillwell Station? I'm on my way there now."

I climbed back into the train and headed that way, my mind racing. I wasn't allowed to check my phone while I was driving, and the suspense was making me a nervous wreck. I still hadn't figured out exactly what had happened to my son. Then I realized that I was rocking back and forth, trying to will the train to go faster. I could feel the anxiety building up inside me. When I arrived at the station, I was alarmed to see Ben standing in the office waiting for me. "What are you doing up here? You can't be in here. I'll get in

1

trouble. I told you to meet me downstairs." I was furious that he was breaking the rules at my job.

"Gwen, it's OK. They let me in. You won't be in trouble. I told them that you needed to get home."

I was still confused, and I had a strange feeling in my stomach. When we got downstairs, I started questioning him nonstop. "What's going on? Did you hear anything? What happened to Eric?"

He said, "We're headed to the hospital to see him. He should be there now."

"Hospital? What do you mean he should be there? I don't understand! We need to call somebody to find out exactly what happened!"

"Make sure to put your seatbelt on," he said.

"I have my seatbelt on. I just—" Just then his phone rang. I couldn't hear what the person on the other end was saying, but I could tell by the look on his face that it was bad. "Was that about Eric?"

"Yeah, he's there, so we're going to the hospital to see him now."

I tried to calm myself down. "OK, but what did they say?" He was silent. "Is anything wrong with my son? Tell me! Tell me!"

He looked at me, and I saw tears streaming down his face, something I'd never seen before. I was truly getting scared.

"Gwen, Eric is dead."

I don't remember much after that. He told me later I was flailing my arms and legs, trying to kick the door open and bust out the window. I was a mother in pain. He had to turn on the automatic locks to keep me safe. He had tried to reason with me: "Gwen, we will be there soon! Please leave the door alone!"

I'm not sure what was going through my mind, but I do recall thinking that if I could just get out of the car, I could run faster. I could get to my son. I could help him. My boy needed me. My mind was spinning. This couldn't be happening again. It couldn't be real. I couldn't have lost another child. There had to be some explanation.

On the way to the hospital, Ben tried to get assistance from a police officer. He was of no help, but at the time I didn't understand his reluctance. When we got to the hospital, they told Ben that I couldn't go in since I was obviously in no condition to see Eric. We went home so that we could try to find out what had happened. I remember sitting in the living room just feeling numb, not sure what was going on. Nothing was making sense to me. Everything around me seemed to be moving really fast and in slow motion all at once. It was like my senses couldn't comprehend what was happening around me.

I tried a trick that I had heard about on some TV show. I needed something to focus on, so I chose Eric's graduation photo, which was displayed on the wall in a neat row along with mine and those of my two other biological children, Emery and Ellisha. As I looked at Eric's beaming face, I remembered how proud I was of my firstborn that day. Then I focused on my breathing. As I continued to focus on the photo, I took a deep breath, held it for a few seconds, and exhaled. Then I turned my attention to my right foot. Still looking at the photo, I squeezed it and then relaxed it, then moved on to the left foot. This sounded silly when I heard it, but at this moment it gave me a sense of control. My mind was focused on one small task, and that brought me a brief sense of calm.

Just then the front door slammed shut, yanking me back into the harsh world I was trying to escape. Family members kept coming by in a steady stream, and that damn front door slammed each time, causing me to jump in my seat. The relaxation was short lived, and once again I was a nervous wreck. My mind was like a pressure cooker as I relived the moments leading up to this point. I wasn't sure how much more I could take.

We kept getting bits of information. Police. Cigarettes. Chokehold. Sidewalk. Something happened over on Bay Street in Staten Island, and news in the community travels real fast, especially bad news. I couldn't make much sense of it, but I knew that something horrible had happened because news reporters began showing up at the house. Just a few hours ago, I was driving the train at work, and now there were reporters outside, all wanting to talk with us. It was a whirlwind, and everything was happening so fast that the family wasn't sure what to do, what to say, or who to talk to.

Finally, my brother-in-law announced that he thought we should let one reporter in and ask him to print exactly what we told him. That way he felt that at least we would have some control over the message that would apparently be all over the news judging by the number of crews that had gathered outside, constantly asking us for comment whenever someone would enter or leave. The reporter who was chosen came in and talked to each of us. We gave our statements and asked him whether he would show us what he planned to print. He seemed very respectful and promised that he would write exactly what we had said. We thanked him for doing that and walked him to the door. Just then he stopped and turned around.

"There's one thing that I want to tell you before you see it on the news tomorrow morning. We have it as an exclusive."

"What do you mean?" Ben asked.

"There's a video of the incident."

Back in the day, we referred to the downtown area as "South Brooklyn," and that's where I grew up. I was born in 1949 at Cumberland Hospital on 39 Auburn Place. That beautiful, historic building located near Fort Greene Park was also the birthplace of some famous folks like Michael Jordan, Mike Tyson, and Spike Lee. The hospital served the community well, and practically everyone in the area was born there, knew someone who worked there, or had a relative pass away there. It closed in the 1980s and is now used by the city as a homeless shelter.

When I would walk by there as a child, I would often imagine all the events that took place inside those red brick walls. I'd smile thinking about the adorable little babies that were being born to excited, hopeful young couples. I'd imagine what it was like when people were getting sad news about being sick, and how excited they would be when they got better. Then I'd get a slight shiver thinking about the ones who passed away, hoping that wouldn't happen in my family for a long time. It was like we were all on loan from that place, like we were given the gift of life, sent out into the world, only to return one day, at the end.

I was always something of a quiet little girl. I tended to keep to myself, not talking too much or making a big fuss about things. It wasn't because I didn't have ideas, because I did. Thoughts were always dancing around inside my head as I tried to figure out how the world worked and how I fit into it. I would watch all the children screaming and playing in the streets, mothers sitting on stoops laughing, crying, and living their lives for everyone to see. That just wasn't me. I preferred to think things through first, to observe others and learn from them. I felt more comfortable that way. I would rather wait for things to come to me.

My mother, Lula Mae, and father, Joseph Flagg, raised us to be polite and respectful. I had two sisters, Sharon and Marilyn, and two brothers, Joseph and James. With five kids, you could say it was always a busy household. Not only that, but we also had extended family nearby, and that number increased quite a bit as the years went on. I also had a best friend named Vernice. I had known her since we were babies, and she ended up living with us as well. I guess my parents figured that one more child wasn't going to make much difference. Most people assumed that she was my sister because we were inseparable. That was fine by me because my parents taught us that family was everything. It was important to stick together and be there for each other. And by taking in Vernice when she needed it, they had reinforced the importance of unity. My folks always tried to lead by example.

My father was a Baptist minister, and most of my mother's and father's siblings lived on the same street with us. My father's sisters all had family nicknames—Sweets, Doll Baby, Baby-Mae, Lil' Sister, Cora, and Maude—and he had two brothers, Wilbert and Eugene. My mother had three sisters in the area—Alberta, Martha-Lee, and Catherine—and a brother named James who stayed back in North Carolina. Throughout my childhood, our extended family lived either on the same street or just a few blocks away. What fun we had with so many of my cousins always around. They all played an important role in my childhood and adult life.

In our neighborhood, we were surrounded by all types of people, from all over the world. None of us had a lot of money, but we did have our unique heritage, and we all cherished it like gold. There were the Irish, Italians, Germans, and of course Black folks. It was very much a melting pot and a good way to learn about different cultures by going to school with the other children. We were all neighbors and tried to treat each other with respect. While people were proud of their heritage and didn't hide it, out on the streets we were the same. We were a family. Grownups looked out for each other, and children were raised to respect the adults.

That doesn't mean things were perfect by any means. There would, of course, be fights and arguments, but they would usually blow over. Some of the boys would fight in the street occasionally, settling some type of disagreement. My grandmother would get very upset. "Those boys need to stop that before it gets out of hand," she would say. I told her, "It's OK, Grandma. They will act foolish and when it's over they will be friends again." She still didn't like it, especially if there was a Black boy fighting a White one. When she was growing up, she was always worried that the Black kid would be the one in trouble. I could tell that it really upset her.

My parents were from the South and very proud of their roots. Daddy grew up on a farm in Sparta, Georgia. He didn't get past the third grade because his family needed him to work, and that left little time for school. My mother was from Greensboro, North Carolina, and she grew up with a love of cooking. People from all over our Brooklyn neighborhood would ask what we were having for supper each night. They loved hearing about the southern dishes Mama would cook, hoping to get invited over for a meal, which they often were.

Our frequent block parties were about fellowship and fun. The mothers would bring covered dishes for the others to try as the kids played stickball or splashed water on each other under the hot August sun. We didn't realize that things were so different in other parts of the country. Of course, as people of color, we heard about the civil rights movement and what was happening in the South, but in our community, discrimination and racial intolerance wasn't a big issue, at least to me. I'm sure Mama and Daddy saw things differently, but as a child I felt happy and secure.

People often talk about their past in such glowing terms and carry on about how simple things were back then, and I do understand why that happens. In our complex world today, we deal with so much technology—the internet, cell phones, GPS tracking—it's everywhere. It has taken over our homes, our cars, and our lives. These conveniences certainly make life easier in some ways, but in others I'm not so sure.

In our neighborhood, the outside was our internet and shouting down the block usually worked better than any phone ever could. I would keep my treasures—a few pennies and some cheap trinkets—in an old cigar box that I'd found on the sidewalk. I also really liked playing with paper dolls. We couldn't afford the fancy books of perforated clothes with folding tabs that held them on the doll, so I would cut out my own from old newspapers or magazines. Sometimes Vernice and I would go to the five-and-ten store to look at the shiny toys, hoping we could buy something brand new one day.

On special occasions, we'd go on an errand with Mama and even take the bus. I loved the clanging sounds as I dropped the three nickels into the metal box and carefully walked down the aisle, climbing on the seat by Mama. Then, especially during the summer when everyone was outside, I would crawl over Mama's lap and press my face against the window, fascinated by the scenes playing out all over the city. I loved seeing other families talking and laughing, all hoping to catch a mild breeze to provide some relief from the punishing heat that arose from the asphalt. No one had air-conditioning, so during the day the houses and apartments were like ovens, trapping the heat inside, noisy metal fans working overtime but providing only minimal relief.

We lived in the same general neighborhood throughout my childhood, so we had lots of friends and family in the area. Our extended family continued to grow, so we felt at home no matter whose house we went to. Most of us lived on Warren Street, and there were always other kids to play with and a gathering happening every weekend. It seemed like someone was always cooking

something on a grill, sending spicy aromas all over the neighborhood. I felt fortunate that we had such a good life. We struggled
to pay the bills from time to time just like everyone else, but with
family to lean on, we always managed. In 1967, I graduated from
John Adams High School in Queens located near an area called
Ozone Park. The school, built in 1927, was a beautiful three-story
building with the cafeteria in the basement. Just like the neighborhoods around there, the student population was very diverse, with
all races blending together, all waiting for the bell to ring at the end
of the day so we could get outside.

I was always a pretty good student, usually As and Bs, especially
in math. I liked reading and studying, and it came easy for me, so
I didn't have to work at it like some of the other kids did. It was
exciting to learn about other places around the country. I'd imagine
what it would be like to live somewhere else, but then I'd think I
was being silly: I'd never leave all my family here in South Brooklyn.
Not only that, but I'd also met a boy named Bernard Garner during
my senior year, and I was in love.

He had gone to Westinghouse High School in Brooklyn and was
a few years older than me. However, things were a little complicated
at first because he already had three children. I was eighteen when
we got involved, and it was a package deal; I had an instant family. I
hadn't expected to have children around so quickly, but it seemed to
work out perfectly. Bernard's ex was very understanding, so the kids
were a part of our life from day one. There were two girls (Lorraine
Margaret and Ella Lynette) and a boy (Elliott Bernard), all under
ten years old. Soon they were my stepchildren, and it was a role that
I was born to fill. Being a mother and taking care of those kids just
came naturally to me. Motherhood fit me like a glove. I took right
to it.

Bernard and his first wife had gotten married very young, ages
fifteen and sixteen. She had gotten pregnant, and their parents
insisted on it. The union lasted about five years. I was happy to
help raise those three children, and they were at our house every
weekend. Today, they have children of their own who consider me
their grandmother, just as if they were my own grandbabies. People

I knew from way back know I'm not the natural grandmother, but others don't realize I'm the "stepgrandmother." They just consider me "Grandma." That's how close I became with those children and their mother. I treated them really well and they always respected me, even though their mother was still alive. She and I maintained a good relationship and never had any real problems.

That was probably because when she and Bernard decided to go their separate ways, there was no harshness. She had chosen to be with someone else, and he wanted to be with me. We always got along, and she would call me to say, "I want to bring the children over for the weekend. Is it OK?" She would call me instead of calling him. Of course, I always said, "Sure."

Even now, her sisters and brothers, many of whom live in Washington, DC, will call to ask me if I can visit when I'm in town. They tell me, "Our sister always said you were a great person. She couldn't have found a better stepmother for the children." A lot of people thought that was an unusual relationship, but that's just the way it developed. It wasn't by accident, though. I was dedicated to making my new family work, just as I had learned from my parents. At the end of the day, family was all you had to rely on, so you'd better have a strong foundation.

When my own children were born, the stepchildren used to tease my kids and say, "Oh, she was our mother before she was your mother." They really loved each other and always called each other brother and sister. Bernard's first wife had two other children, and those children were close with my children as well. Bernard's sisters Hazel, Frieda, Constance, and Edna were also around, so it was like one big family. I was really proud that it happened like that. Often, there was a lot of dysfunction with extended families, but not with us.

While I loved those children so much, I was very excited when my first child was born on September 15, 1970, in Long Island College Hospital in the Cobble Hill section of Brooklyn. Since the other children were getting older, it was wonderful to have a newborn of my own to raise. I had been around plenty of babies growing up, but it's true that when you have one of your own, it's so special. All those feelings I had wondered about came true many times over. I couldn't believe this little one would be dependent on me to protect him from harm. It was a responsibility I took very seriously. I often whispered to him, "I'll never let anything happen to you, little man." Bernard's first son already had his name, so we changed it up. We named him Eric Bernard Garner.

I first noticed Eric's asthma when he was about seven months old. He was my firstborn, so I wasn't sure if I was being overprotective, but I could tell he was having trouble breathing. It was cute at the beginning, how he would purse his lips together as he stared at me with those big brown eyes. It almost looked like he was trying to speak. Then I guess that mother's intuition kicked in because something didn't feel right. He would gasp for air constantly. It wasn't a slow, steady breathing pattern. Instead, it was like he was gulping for air, as if he had just come from being underwater. I told my husband something was wrong. We took him to the hospital right away.

Sure enough, the doctor agreed that there was an issue. Not only that, but he also informed me that my little Eric had to stay in the hospital. "We need to monitor him," he told me. I couldn't fathom leaving my baby there. At that time, visitors were only allowed during posted hours. There was no option to stay overnight and camp out beside my baby. I had to leave him there and go home with no idea of how long he would have to stay. It reminded me of the times I'd pass by Cumberland Hospital and think about the helpless newborns inside.

Every night when I left the hospital after visiting hours and got in bed, I would toss and turn. I just couldn't sleep. It felt like a part of me was missing. After a long labor and several months of doting on my sweet baby, there was now a void, an emptiness, and it was tearing me apart. I had promised him that I would keep him safe, and it felt like I was failing. At night when the house was still, I would instinctively twitch every time there was a creak or settling noise. I knew I wouldn't be able to relax until Eric was back at home.

The diagnosis indicated that he had an upper respiratory infection and would require more treatment and monitoring. In fact, they ended up keeping him there for almost five months. I couldn't believe he had to be there that long, but the doctors wanted to make sure he was able to breathe unassisted, which I understood, but I wasn't happy about it. I went there every single day and worked it into my routine. Any time they had visitors' hours, I was there. There was a backyard area where the sick children were allowed to play and have visitors if they were feeling up to it. Of course, my husband, parents, and other family members came as well, but I didn't miss a single day. I couldn't. I knew it was important to bond with my child while he was young, so those few hours we spent together each day in the garden were very precious to me.

My little boy looked so vulnerable in that special crib where they monitored him constantly, but I was sure that any day now they would let him come home. They just kept saying, "Not yet, Gwen. Not yet." In September 1971 I told the doctor, "You know his birthday is on the 15th. We want to have a party for him at home. You have to let me take him. It's his first birthday. Please?" He thought for a minute and said, "OK, Gwen, you can take him home for the weekend for his birthday. Then I want to see you back here on Monday." I was so happy and excited that I would have agreed to anything. "Yes, of course," I said, as my mind raced. My baby would be coming home!

It was so interesting watching Eric as we made our way out of the hospital. His little eyes popped open wide at all of the city noises—the cars, trucks, sirens. It was so new to him and a big change from the controlled environment of that tiny crib. I can't describe how complete I felt with him at home. When all of the family came over for his first birthday party, I was so happy that I could barely focus on the festivities. My baby had come back, and the whole family was there to celebrate.

Any milestone event like a first birthday gave our family yet another reason to come together and celebrate. So when I found out my baby was coming home, I wasted no time decorating and coordinating his party. We had such a fun day celebrating Eric and his health. Despite that asthma, he was out of the hospital on his birthday and smearing cake all over his face as we all watched and laughed. I couldn't have been happier.

That Monday, as promised, I did take him back, but he only ended up staying a week or so longer until he was ready to come home for good. We were provided with a breathing machine that he needed to use daily, and the doctor told me there would be a lot of restrictions. Also, as Eric got older, if he didn't improve dramatically, he might have to go to a special school or even be homeschooled. He probably wouldn't be able to play sports, either. I nodded slowly as the doctor gave us this news. I was ready to do whatever I had to do to keep my boy healthy.

By the time he was around three years old, Eric seemed to have improved a great deal. He even went to school—first at Head Start in October 1973, then to Bethel Daycare. Once he started attending elementary school at PS 32 in 1976, his condition was almost unnoticeable. He would have an attack every now and then, but for the most part his breathing seemed under control. He was even able to eventually play sports and run around like the other children. Still, I was cautious, and when he was at school I asked the teachers about him to make sure he wasn't overdoing it. Everyone assured me that he was fine. The doctor was amazed by his recovery and said he'd never seen anything quite like it. It was a miracle. Eric could breathe.

That was a big relief for me because two years after Eric was born, I had another son named Emery. With a toddler and an infant along with the stepchildren, I sure did have my hands full, but it was a good feeling. Bernard was working hard to provide for us, and I worked too when I could. Fortunately, Emery did not have any immediate health issues, so while he was very little I was able to watch Eric start to become his own person.

Eric learned how to love and share with other people as a small child. He was very personable and trusting. He would always go along with the ideas of other kids because he was so friendly he thought everyone was that way. I used to tell him, "Eric, everybody's not your friend." On many occasions he would bring a kid home from school. "Ma, they wanted to beat my friend up, so I brought him home. He's going to eat dinner with us." That was just the type of person he was. If he found out that someone had betrayed him, he would be heartbroken and wouldn't want to speak to them. I did my best to educate him and teach him about how the world worked. I'd say, "Things like that happen." He'd say, "No, he was supposed to be my friend." It was just inconceivable to him that a person could betray his trust. Since he was so loyal and trusting, he thought everyone was. There were some things he had to learn on his own.

One thing that was undeniable was his love of other people. He had the ability to connect with almost anyone. He especially looked forward to holidays, particularly Christmas. Christmas was the most magical time of year for him. As a child, he couldn't wait to see which toys he got. "I know we got something great," he would tell the other kids. I would never let them see anything before the big day. I was very careful to make it special, like my mother had done with us. On Christmas morning, all of their little eyes would light up, and I would grab my Instamatic camera, taking picture after picture as the square flash on top twirled until it burned out.

The kids just loved the spirit of being around each other, and we never missed a family gathering. I remember there was one cookout that Eric missed because he was in the hospital for his asthma. Everyone asked, "Where is Eric? Eric's not coming?" He was always the life of the party, so they looked forward to seeing him. He always wanted everyone to be happy.

For being such a skinny child, Eric was always a big eater. He wanted to get his share, but he would make sure everyone else had some, too. My mother used to say, "I'd rather clothe him than feed him." Speaking of my mother, those kids sure did love to go stay with their grandparents. Eric would tell me, "We love to go over to Grandma's house because it's like a big campout. She lets us all sleep in the living room and she puts sheets up like tents and even brings us food in there. We love that!" He was so excited describing it all to me. My mother was always coming up with things like that to keep them entertained. I can tell you she never did that for us when we were little, but I was learning that grandchildren are special and spoiling them is part of the fun.

They used to always say that Grandma loved Eric the best. I said, "Why do you all say that? She treats you all very well and lets all of you come over at the same time." They'd say, "Yeah, but you can just tell Eric is her favorite." All the other kids in the family said that, too, but I couldn't see it. To me, she treated them the same, but they were adamant about it. They were mostly just kidding around because there was love enough for all of them.

On September 28, 1975, I finally had a girl, and I named her Ellisha, keeping with the theme of starting their names with the letter E. Being around the boys for four years, it was fun to have a little girl I could dote on. With my parents and Bernard's as well, we had plenty of help and support. Our little family was making its way in the world. By the time I was twenty-six, we had two adorable boys and now the baby girl I'd always wanted. Watching her grow and change was so exciting for me. To see her little personality start to emerge, I just couldn't imagine anything better. The boys had become very close and pitched in to help take care of their little sister.

Bernard had been working steadily to bring in some money, which at times was very tough. Plus he had the added responsibility of his other three children, but we were making it work as a family. He suffered from high blood pressure, and all of a sudden, out of the blue, he had a stroke in 1975. He totally lost the ability to talk and was confined to a hospital bed at home. A therapist visited regularly to help restore his speech. As in all times of trouble, family came to our aid and offered any help they could. My parents were even more helpful than usual, taking baby Ellisha and the boys as much as I needed so that I could nurse my husband back to health. I was sure that if we were patient and followed the doctor's advice carefully, my husband would be back home in no time. The children really missed their daddy.

For a time, things did seem to improve. Bernard was making strides in his speech and gaining some of his strength back, but it just wasn't God's plan. He lost his grip on life and slipped away from us in 1976. I was left with Eric at five years old, Emery at almost four, and Ellisha at just four months. Bernard Garner was thirty-three years old when he died.

The funeral took place on a Friday, February 13, and the next day, Valentine's, I took to my bed. I just couldn't handle the blanket of sadness. One day, my mother was watching Ellisha while Eric and Emery stayed with me. After my father finished work, he came over to talk to the kids and make sure everything was all right. When the door opened, Eric said, "Hi, Grandpa. Mommy didn't feed us today." When I overheard that, I realized that he was right: I hadn't fed my own children. I was afraid my father would be upset, but he wasn't. He said, "Oh, you didn't eat anything?" Eric said, "Well, I made cereal for me and Emery and we had juice, but Mommy didn't get up and cook our bacon and eggs like usual."

I just lay there listening in on their conversation, still in disbelief that I had been so consumed by grief that I wasn't caring for the children properly. My father went into my refrigerator and took out a chicken, cut it up, fried it, and fixed their dinner. "I'm fixing y'all dinner and putting some in the refrigerator so tomorrow y'all will have some too," I heard him say.

It was at that moment when I realized that I needed to get up out of bed and move on with my life—our lives. I couldn't have lapses like that with small children to raise. I was going into a depression and hadn't realized what was happening until Eric's pronouncement snapped me out of it. My father understood how distraught I was, so without saying much about it he would drop by every day at about the same time to check up on us. He was very calm and supportive, but he was also letting me know that someone needed to be there for the kids. I got the message loud and clear. I needed to be strong for them, and I really appreciated him for making sure I understood that.

Then I started to hear rumors about my husband, and it was disturbing. People in the streets were talking about how he had a drug problem and that's what eventually caused his heart problems. I was shocked because I had no idea that evil had taken hold of my family. I suppose I was so consumed with raising small children that it never occurred to me that Bernard was under the influence. It was shocking to hear, and I realized that I would probably never know exactly what had happened to him.

With my husband gone, my parents stepped in much more, coming to get the children almost every weekend and taking them to their new home on Coney Island. Then on Sunday, after church, they would deliver them back to my place in Brooklyn. That gave me the time I needed to grieve and get myself together. Bernard's parents, Ella and Elliott Garner, also helped when they could. The kids understood death to a certain point, but they didn't really comprehend what had happened. I explained to them, "Your father is gone forever." After a month or so Eric asked, "Is it forever yet? Is he coming home now?" I told him, "No, he's never coming home."

I took them to the cemetery once, and while we were standing around talking I saw Emery out of the corner of my eye. He was trying to pull the plaque off his father's grave. I said, "What are you doing?" He said, "This is a stone. I think it's too heavy on my daddy."

That loss was a lot for our young family to handle. At first, I just didn't even want to face the world without Bernard by my side, despite the things I had heard about his last days. We had started this journey together, and I felt cheated out of our future. What kept me going was being able to see glimpses of him in the children. As the boys got older, I noticed it more with them. There would be a mannerism or a word that reminded me of Bernard and it would make me smile. I realized that we were all going to make it as long as we had each other.

# Chapter 2

## Finding Strength

Success is to be measured not so much by the position that one has reached in life as by the obstacles which he has overcome while trying to succeed.

—Booker T. Washington

BY 1977, WE WERE LIVING IN the Gowanus area of Brooklyn where the neighborhood had a remote feel, like we were on our own island within the city. There were modest rowhouses surrounded by large industrial warehouses and a canal that was almost two miles long and at one point was the nation's busiest. Unfortunately, it was also unregulated, so by the time we lived there, it was very polluted from the area factories and rumored to be a mob dumping ground. The color of the water got so bad that we called it "Lavender Lake." In the summertime, you could smell it from blocks away.

One of the things I liked about the neighborhood was that, just as when I was growing up, the people were very diverse. There were Blacks, Whites, Asians, all different types of folks. I liked that my kids were exposed to other people and other cultures. My grandmother's focus on racism always stuck with me. I felt fortunate that we didn't seem to face that issue nearly as much as she had.

I was twenty-six when my husband passed away, and even with the help of grandparents on both sides and other family, it was not easy for us. The money Bernard brought into the house wasn't a lot, and it wasn't always steady income, but it was something. Without him, I felt like I was drowning financially. I didn't feel right moving our family into Gowanus public housing and living on government assistance, but I realized that I didn't have any other options. We referred to it as "the luxury projects." The fact was that I couldn't earn enough money on my own to support all of us, which included not only my three kids but also my three stepchildren: Lorraine, Ella, and Elliott Bernard.

Taking care of them by myself was beyond difficult, but I was determined to make sure all the children had a fair shot at a good life away from the dangers of the street. Living in that small apartment with my three children was an exercise in patience and organization. In addition, my stepdaughter, Ella (who we called Lynette), lived with us and the other two visited often. I worked hard to keep everyone on their schedule and make sure they got along under the crowded circumstances. Without a lot of money, I did the best I could. Despite the crowded conditions, I didn't mind it so much. I was raised with so many relatives around all the time that it felt natural. My parents and other family members pitched in often to help. That was one thing I could always count on. We would all come together when one of us needed help.

No matter what struggles we had to overcome, I was very focused on everyone getting a good education and taking school seriously. My stepchildren (whom I just referred to as my kids) were older, so they started school first. Then Eric began public school in 1976, and in 1979 he was bused to PS 27 across town. Emery began school two years later, and then Ellisha. Finally having them all in school allowed me to work and start earning a little money. That gave me hope that one day we would be able to afford a place of our own.

After high school, my first job was with the New York Telephone Company, and then I worked at the New York Stock Exchange and at the World Trade Center. Once Bernard passed, I managed to go back to school to get a degree. I knew I was going to need one to care for the children properly. I finally got a job at the post office and was promoted to account technician. Working there helped me start to get on my feet and provide for my family. Later I was able to get the position with the New York City Transit Authority.

As the years passed, despite the difficulties, one of the true joys for me was watching the children develop and grow. Their personalities really started to come out, and as a mother, it was wonderful to be a part of that. When I had time I dated sporadically, but I didn't have a serious boyfriend for a while, so it was mostly me and the children.

With the boys being just two years apart in age, as they grew up it was hard to remember who was oldest because Emery saw himself as the man of the house. He had more of a take-charge personality, and he was always getting into something. He would often come home with an animal he had found somewhere. One day he brought a garden snake into the house as a pet. I sometimes gave in to him because he did step up and assume responsibility for the family. He was a very bright child and a natural leader.

Eric was much more laid back; he was not as intense and driven as Emery. With Eric it was more about relationships with others and making friends. As he got older, he was also more politically aware than the rest of us. Eric would watch the news and read the paper, always talking about what the government was up to and keeping us informed.

The one thing that Eric and Emery agreed on was that they needed to watch over their baby sister and help her to make good choices. Ellisha complained that they were overprotective, and I'm sure it felt like that to her, but they did not want her getting mixed up with the wrong crowd. They were strict about when she could go out of the house and always had to know where she was going and who else would be there.

When my stepchildren got older and moved out, I thought things would get easier because there were fewer children to care for, but then my brother passed away. I took in his three children—Stevie, Kimberly, and Lil Joe—because they didn't have anywhere else to go and I was very close to them. I loved them like my own anyway and wanted to do what I could to help. The other children probably weren't too happy about having to share their apartment and their mother again, but they realized that was what we had to do to get by. When one of us needed help, everyone pitched in without question.

I did such a good job of shielding the children from our impoverished conditions that they often made comments about how rich we were. I said, "How can we be rich? We live in the projects!" It was true that our Christmas celebrations were a sight to behold. It's surprising that even without a lot of money, I was able to scrimp and save throughout the year to make sure they had a special day. One time, a friend of mine brought over some money and used them to decorate our Christmas tree. It had a $50 bill on the top and tens, fives, and ones on the lower branches. No one had ever seen anything like it, and the children stared at it for hours, never daring to touch the dollars that tempted them.

Eric was very much into sports as a kid, especially basketball, and when he got older his attention shifted to football. I was always cautious about athletics because of his past health problems, but he could run. Eric wasn't in the Boy Scouts, but he was in the cadets. He went to a local center where they taught how to march in formation. I was always impressed that he wasn't afraid to try new things like that.

We were in public housing until Eric was in the ninth grade, and I was excited when he went to the same junior high that I had attended. He had been attending PS 27 on Huntington and Columbia Streets in the Red Hook section of Brooklyn, which is where a lot of kids from the projects went. After he graduated from PS 27, he found out he would be attending MS 51 on Fifth Avenue in Park Slope. He came home and said, "I'm going to be going to 51. Mom, didn't you say you went to that middle school?" I said, "Yeah I did."

In fact, I had a great time attending William Alexander Middle School and got good grades. There was a diverse mix of students, and they offered lots of programs to keep the children interested in learning. It was mostly working-class folks when I went there, but today the area has been gentrified and the school is celebrated for its gifted and talented program and its dedication to diversity.

I wondered whether any of my old teachers were still there. When I went back to visit, I found out my vice principal had a new title: "Dean of the Boys." He had the thankless job of chasing us kids off school grounds if we were out there goofing off or playing punchball. When I saw him, I said, "You may not remember me, but my son will be coming here, and you will be his dean." He said, "Oh, yeah, I remember you." I asked where all the teachers were, and most had moved on or retired. We had a nice conversation, and I felt very comfortable with Eric going to the school. I was especially excited when I found out that Eric loved junior high. One of his favorite classes was home economics, where the students learned basic skills like how to cook. The teacher said that any time they were going to cook, Eric would volunteer to help out whenever he was needed. He really flourished in that school.

Don't get me wrong. I'm not saying my son was perfect. Well, he was in my eyes, but I knew that there might be problems in school. In fact, one day he came home and said, "Ma, you gotta come up to the school."

*Oh, no,* I thought, *here it comes. He has gotten into some real trouble.* I remembered some of my classmates who were always acting up, and I hoped Eric would not take that path. I asked, "What did you do?"

He said, "The teacher will tell you, but it wasn't my fault."

"Have you been disrespectful? What is it?"

He said, "No, it wasn't me."

I was not in the mood for any foolishness, and I didn't want to find out that Eric was playing around in class. When I got over to the school, the first thing the teacher said was "It wasn't Eric's fault." I guess she could see that I was a little upset. I did not want to get into the habit of having to take off work for a school visit. Eric's teacher was quick to calm me down. "We were in the cooking class, and we were going to bake cakes. I told all the boys to write down the recipe. Eric was sitting at his desk and writing as he was instructed. I think he had just gotten a haircut." I nodded yes. "Well, this boy came by and popped him in the back of the head. Eric turned around and yelled at the boy. I told them that if anyone throws a lick, they are suspended. Eric looked over at the other boy and then took the cake mix off the table and slung it out of the window. That was his way of getting out his frustration without getting in a fight, but I still had to let you know what happened."

I was relieved that he never really had any trouble in school. Eric would always do his homework; in fact, he would even do it in other classes. In math class, he would do his science homework. In science, he would do his English homework. The teachers would constantly tell him that they appreciated that he kept up with his studies, but he needed to do that at home. When I would ask him if he'd done his homework, he would always say yes, and he would show it to me. Here's what one teacher wrote in his yearbook: *Eric, good luck in high school, work hard, and you will succeed. Remember, if you want to get that piece of paper (diploma) you're going to have to make some changes. You can do it! Remember the T.H.S. code you recited at graduation, it will help you in high school. Mr. Russel.*

In the summer, Eric loved swimming. "Mama, are we going to the pool?" I wasn't crazy about those pools because as a mother I always felt they were dirty, but of course the children did not care. As a compromise, I would let them go once in a while. My mother lived across the street from the beach, so in the summer they went there a lot. They got to visit the beach, and my father took them fishing. They loved experiencing such a different way of life when they visited their grandparents.

While Eric was easygoing and Emery was always looking for a way to begin a career in business, Ellisha was my activist. When she was barely a teenager, she developed a strong interest in justice and the fair treatment of others, especially Black folks. When she was only around twelve years old, she even convinced me to let her go with a friend to march through the streets of Howard Beach to protest the treatment of the White defendants in Michael Griffith's death. I admired her drive and commitment. I was much too reserved to even think about getting involved in something like that. It just wasn't on my radar, but I learned a lot from watching Ellisha.

In 1987 when Eric was seventeen, he graduated from my high school exactly twenty years after I had graduated from there. I was very proud that he chose to attend Ohio Auto Diesel Technical School after high school to learn a trade. My firstborn was going to college! In preparation, I shopped every day leading up to the time for him to leave. I was going back and forth to the store buying pillows, sheets, and even raincoats.

"Ma, why are you buying all this stuff? I don't need no raincoat," Eric said.

"Yes, you do," I insisted.

We were equally excited when it was time to visit the school and see the room he would stay in. I had a cousin in Cleveland who said she would take us over there. We went and stayed at her house, and she drove us to the school the next day. It was a beautiful place, and I couldn't have been more excited for my college student. It was a four-year program, and I was sure he could do it since he had always enjoyed school.

He was studying car mechanics, and when he came home over Christmas break, of course I went overboard to celebrate the holiday with our new college student. He spent the next summer at home and then went back in the fall, but when he returned the next Christmas, he told me he was quitting. We had never imagined that there would be issues with his breathing, but when he worked on cars during the program, the fumes and smells severely triggered his asthma. Unfortunately, he would not be able to follow his dream. I respected his decision, but inside I was crushed. I wanted the best for my children, and that meant a solid education. One thing I do know is that the world is wide, and the world is tough. As young Black adults, they would need every possible advantage to have a fighting chance at a good life. I just hoped his asthma would finally get under control and he could get "off the pump" at some point. I know he didn't like using those inhalers.

It always amused me to see how different my children were. I knew they had their own distinct personalities, but as they matured, their interests did as well. Emery was the artist, and he loved to draw. As a child, one of his favorites was Snoopy, and he continued to develop his talent. He eventually got a job doing some freelance artwork for *Forbes* magazine. Emery was always on his grind and would do anything to earn money. During high school he took many odd jobs, including a stint as a doorman, which he enjoyed because of all the celebrities he would meet. He had big plans for his future, and I couldn't wait to see how far he could go.

In the meantime, Eric worked for Greyhound for a little while and even in some auto mechanic shops, but his asthma returned, and those places weren't good for his health. He loved being involved with cars, but the chemicals and smells didn't agree with him. Eventually, he worked at the Parks Department, and he was a natural thanks to those summers of gardening with his grandfather. Then life changed dramatically in 1988 when Eric got married, and two years later he had his first child. He was a natural father, but supporting a family proved difficult. Without any marketable skills, the most he could hope for were minimum wage jobs that barely paid enough to support one person, much less a family.

I understood his situation completely because I had been through it myself. I had worked various jobs to make money after the children got older, and in 1993 I started at the Metropolitan Transportation Authority as a conductor. It was shift work, mostly overnights, but it was steady money, and I hoped that it showed all the kids how important it was to have a good job. I was trying my best to set a good example for them as a single parent, especially for Ellisha. I wanted her to see that as Black women we can make our own way despite the obstacles.

My Ellisha was very independent and headstrong. I would hear Emery and Eric scold her about making sure she behaved in school and got good grades. Whenever she was in trouble, Emery would warn her, "Keep it up. Look at what everybody else is out here doing and you're not doing anything. You're going to be left behind." He was trying to fill that fatherly role and was genuinely concerned. His words had an effect on her briefly, but then at seventeen she got pregnant and left school to have her daughter. When my granddaughter, Chayla, was born I thought she was the most precious baby, and I was there when she came into the world.

As was typical of their personalities, Eric shrugged off her pregnancy while Emery and her cousin Lil Joe were worried for her and her future. Of course, I was too. Raising a family without a partner was not something I wished on anyone. The struggles and worries had been overwhelming for me, and I didn't want that for her. When she was nineteen, Ellisha and her daughter moved out on their own. She worked in various positions at places like the New York State Division of Veterans Affairs and Philip Morris.

We all go through tough times, and we usually come out on the other side. We learn a valuable lesson about perseverance and determination. I've had my share, but I can honestly say that 1996 was just a horrible year. It started out bad and ended even worse. Someone told me about that trick where you write down a bad memory on a piece of paper and burn it as a way of healing and moving forward. If I had thought of it, I would have written down "1996" and burned it in the biggest fire I could have found. In January of that year, I had to say goodbye to my father, Joseph Flagg. He was the patriarch of our family, the rock, my biggest supporter. He and my mother had helped me raise the children from infancy to adulthood. They welcomed them for weekends and summers and came to my place when I needed them. They were always there until January 31, 1996, when my father passed away.

It had been many years since my husband had transitioned, and I had almost forgotten how painful that gaping hole in the heart can feel. Navigating a landscape that did not include my father was unimaginable. He was such an integral part of the family that his loss was difficult for all of us. That was how the year started out, and in October yet another tragedy befell our family.

Sometimes, as an escape, I would take some money that I had saved and go to the casinos. It was a way to relieve stress and feel that jolt of adrenaline when the alarm went off and lights swirled around in a world of manufactured excitement. On some trips I won and on others I lost, but that feeling of infinite possibility was heady. I couldn't get that feeling anywhere else. My life was structured and routine. Granted, that was by choice. With most of the kids doing their own thing, my focus was on work and seeing everyone on the weekends. Gambling allowed me to escape my everyday life and enter a world of excitement and glamor. Being in the vicinity of high rollers and big money somehow gave me a greater sense of worth. I was there along with everyone else. My wins and losses were not even in their league, but that didn't matter. I had a seat at the table.

These casino trips were a brief diversion, an exotic escape bookended by the realities of life. Winning gave me confidence and boosted my self-esteem. I'd get an electric charge when I won, and that was a feeling I couldn't duplicate while driving a train for the MTA. I had my little tricks too. I'd set my limit before going and would only surpass it if I won small amounts that I would use to continue playing.

In October 1996, Ellisha and I made our way to Atlantic City for one of those casino getaways. She was fun to travel with, and she enjoyed a little gambling as well. However, during this trip, I had an odd sensation; something didn't feel right. I couldn't put my finger on it, but I have always followed my instincts, and something just felt off.

When we returned home, ready to assimilate into regular life again, we got horrible news: Emery had been in Harlem and was shot five times. Apparently, five guys had robbed him and then shot him. Ellisha told me to stay home while she went to the hospital to assess the situation. I appreciated that because my intuition had been right; something *was* wrong. I needed to get myself together. Ellisha told me that when she saw Emery, he looked huge in the small hospital bed and his face was severely swollen. He told her that he was fine, but of course I had to see for myself.

The next day I went to the ICU to see my boy. I couldn't believe how horrible he looked. I knew it would be bad, but he was almost unrecognizable. We both started crying immediately. For me, it was a release of all the anxiety and worry that had gathered in my heart. It was horrible seeing my child in such pain.

Always the protector, Emery told me, "Don't worry. The worst part is over with."

"What do you mean?" I asked. "You have a long way to go. How did this happen?"

"I told you, I was robbed."

Now, I was not as innocent and oblivious as my children often thought. I knew what went on in those streets. It was hard out there, especially for young Black men. Jobs were not easy to come by, and the jobs that were available didn't pay much. I knew it was a frustrating position for my children to be in, but that was their hand in life and it was up to them to play it to the best of their ability.

The brutal attack on Rodney King and the rioting that followed in Los Angeles in 1992 reminded us of the dangers of being Black in America. Police brutality was talked about, but when the chaos and savagery was finally captured on a camcorder, there was undeniable proof of the treatment that we had to endure as Black folks. When those images were transmitted to every living room in the country, it was a wakeup call, especially to Whites, to see how our people were treated. I was fascinated by the fact that someone had been able to film those horrors and expose America's ugly secret.

After those officers were acquitted of the crimes against Mr. King, the crimes that had been caught *on film*, we were all shocked. I could not understand how anyone could look at that and decide that they should not be punished. No one should ever be treated the way Mr. King was. It was like his life was meaningless to them, like he was nobody. How could anyone ever watch a film of such cruelty and not convict the perpetrators?

We all understood why the riots began. I had some familiarity with these issues because of Eric's interest in politics and Ellisha's activism. I was proud of them for their passion and dedication to racial equality, but I was scared too, and that video was what I feared most. As a mother, I couldn't imagine how the King family felt watching that happen to their kin. At the time I didn't think that I'd be able to survive if something like that happened to one of my children.

I had tried to keep the channels of communication with them open as they grew up. We talked about what it was like out in the streets, the brutality and inequality that seemed to become more of an issue with each passing year. I told them that there were things police do to people of color, especially men, and it was important for them to be very careful when they were out in the city. It was the talk all mothers in the Black community are forced to have with their children—an unfortunate tradition.

If any of my children did run into trouble, they would usually tell me about it, saying they hadn't done anything wrong. I knew that it was very possible that they were innocent, but I also knew what teenagers could get into, and I'm sure that sometimes it was warranted. I tried to stress that it was important that they do the right thing. Both of my sons sold drugs when they were young men, though I didn't know it at the time. Of course, they never brought it to the house—they knew better than that—but I started to hear things.

There was a neighbor around the corner who was a conservative type of guy. He was usually quiet, but when he got drunk it was a different story. He would walk through the neighborhood searching for someone to talk to. Actually, that was how we found out a lot of the neighborhood gossip. He was a real talker. One day he came knocking on my door. I wasn't going to open, but I was curious what he would say.

"Gwen," he said with breath that smelled of the devil, "I need to talk to you. I hope you know your son is selling drugs."

Now he had my attention. "Who?" I asked.

"It's Emery. I know for a fact that he's out here selling them drugs and running with that rough crowd. I thought you already knew. Everybody else does."

I guided my tipsy neighbor to the door and said goodnight. I knew he was as drunk as he could be, but I did wonder if what he said was true. A few weeks later, I found myself alone with Emery and knew it was the right time. "So, you're out here selling drugs, huh? You think I don't know what's going on? Remember, that's what took your father out when you were just a toddler. If that's what you are really doing, it will come to light."

He would never admit it to me because he didn't want to disappoint me, but I knew I was right. Emery ended up getting arrested a few times. Eric also had a few run-ins with the law. Eric had been arrested for pot possession in 1988 and had a few more incidents over the years. I would tell both of them that if they went to jail, I would not come to see them. I was not coming down there because they knew I had a phobia about those bars. I did not what to hear that heavy metallic clang behind me as the bars closed, locking me inside. Despite my fears, of course I went, and I helped them if I could. If they had to serve some time, I wrote them letters and sent care packages like they were in camp, but I didn't like what they had done. I was so upset they would choose that road in life. Later, they would say they didn't mean to hurt me. They never really used hard drugs that I knew of, but they did sell them to earn money. I never liked that, but I also realized that there wasn't much I could do.

I understood the struggle that young Black men face when it comes time to go out on their own. In too many places, racism and preconceived stereotypes prevent them from being able to find decent jobs. They are expected to be the provider for their family, but that becomes difficult when they can't get a job that pays a decent wage. Being young and impatient, they find other ways to make more money, even when they know it's not right. I'm not an expert, and I don't know how that cycle got started, but to create real change we need to come together to find a way to stop it.

When Emery was in the hospital that October, I was sure that it had something to do with drugs and hanging around the wrong people, but the only thing I could do at that point was help him get better. He was twenty-four years old and his own man. I would give my opinion, but it was his life to lead. Once he was able to move around, he was on the go again. He took another trip upstate with a girl he was seeing. I wasn't sure exactly what was going on, but I knew that Ellisha was concerned as well. Emery did like his wine and Hennessy, and Ellisha warned him to go easy because he was still healing.

After he got back from that trip, he seemed to be feeling a little better, and he was back to being a baller, showing everyone that he could earn that paper. One way that he tried to placate us when we asked too many questions was to buy things. He paid for Ellisha's room to be painted and even got her pink carpet. He did other things around the house, too, and his latest promise was that he would buy me a new washing machine. Lord knows that I needed one, but I was not interested in dirty money, and I expressed that. He assured me that I was worrying for nothing.

On December 8, 1996, I came home from work at 6:00 a.m., as usual, to find that the family had gathered at my apartment. I felt my stomach flip-flop inside me as I pushed through the front door. "Where's my mother?" I thought maybe something happened to Mama after we'd already lost Daddy. I was so scared. My sister Sharon told me to sit down, and I said, "No, just tell me what happened. Something bad has happened, hasn't it?" She couldn't do it, so Ellisha told me three words that changed my life forever: "Emery is dead."

You know what that moment felt like? It was as if I had been swallowed up by an ocean wave, like I had been smothered with so much force that I couldn't move. Like the undercurrent was pulling me out to sea forever. They said that I let out a bloodcurdling scream that was so full of pain that everyone broke down crying. I don't remember that. I just kept picturing little Emery growing up, taking charge of the family, comforting me when I was stressed or upset about something. Picturing him like that was the only way I could cope. I just used my memory to push reality off into a dark corner.

Ellisha and the others handled the funeral arrangements because I could barely function. I wasn't sleeping or eating. I didn't talk to anyone, didn't go out, and didn't go to work. It was December, so my house was fully decorated as usual in anticipation of our favorite day of the year. After I got that news, Christmas lost its meaning for me. How could I celebrate when one of my own children had been taken from me? It was simple—I couldn't. The fact was that I couldn't let him go. I was not willing to accept it, because I knew that once I did that meant it was real, and I wasn't sure I could survive that.

Much later, Ellisha and the others gave me the details about what had happened. They told me more about some of the things he had done. He had been swallowed up by the dark side of life on the streets. It was a side he never allowed me to see. Apparently, his trip upstate with the lady was not just a vacation but also a "business opportunity." He had said that he needed to pick up some things and would be right back. Then Ellisha got a call from a friend of

Emery's and he was crying. He told her that Emery had died in his sleep. Ellisha was livid. "What was y'all doing? Did he drink alcohol? He was still healing!"

Ellisha called the local police, and they told her that they couldn't give her information over the phone, but they confirmed that her brother had passed away and someone needed to come identify the body. Ellisha called her uncle, who was a cop, and he went up there with Eric and cousin Stevie. They found out that my son, my little Emery, had been shot once in the back of the head. I still can't make sense of that statement. I see the words, but together they don't mean anything to me. Emery will always be my son, and I won't think of him in any other way. I can't.

I had just spoken to Emery before I went to work that night. He had a son and told me that he had put all his boy's Christmas toys on layaway. "I know you told me you need a new washing machine, so I'm buying you one for Christmas," he reminded me. I said, "Oh really?" After his death I tried my best to find the store that had those toys on layaway. I know it didn't make sense, but I thought that if I could find them and get them, I would somehow have a piece of Emery. I would have the last things he bought, things he had put thought into. I called and visited every store I could think of. Other family members told me to give up, that maybe there wasn't a store, maybe there weren't any toys, but I didn't believe them. I still don't.

The only way I was able to cope was to shut down. It was the only thing I could control. I fell into a depression that was as dark and scary as any hell could ever be. I lost more than sixty pounds because I just didn't have an interest in food, or anything else for that matter. Eric was destroyed by the news, too. He tried to be stoic and strong, but he had moments when I could see that he was hurting. Someone had murdered his brother, my son. It was incomprehensible. Eric wasn't the vengeful type, but he was definitely angry about it.

Eventually, Eric did get better, and talking to him even helped me get to a place where we could at least acknowledge what had happened. It was still a tender subject, and I could only touch on it briefly and then move on, like a finger on a hot stove. I felt that if I lingered too long, the pain would come back again, even stronger. I was just glad that I had Ellisha and Eric close by. We found out that the police caught the man who was responsible on another charge and he was locked up. It wasn't really the closure I thought it would be, though, because it didn't alter the fact that my life had been changed.

Emery was gone.

# Chapter 3

# My Son Can't Breathe

Hate is too great a burden to bear. It injures the hater more than it injures the hated.

—Coretta Scott King

By the spring of 1997, I began to gradually emerge from my grief coma. With the support of my family, I got back to work, and it felt good to be in a routine again. I functioned much better with that structure because it gave purpose to a life that had been in freefall. Another good thing that happened was that Mr. Benjamin Carr came back into my life. I had met him in 1979 when he was working on the windows of our apartment in the projects.

He told me, "If you fix me lunch, I'll make sure your windows get put in tomorrow."

I knew he was flirting, but Lord knows I needed those drafty windows fixed. I said, "You can't do that. We have to wait our turn."

"I can do it," he promised. "And I will."

The next day, I fixed lunch for him, his brother, and a couple of other guys. My husband had been gone for a while, so it was nice to have some attention like that. Ben and I got along well and talked all through lunch. After they left, I didn't think I'd hear from him any time soon.

He came back a couple of days later and said, "I talked to the boss and he said we can put your windows in now."

I was surprised because I figured he was just doing that talk men do sometimes. "What do you mean?" I asked.

"Don't worry. It's all taken care of," he assured me.

I found out years later that he had told his boss some crazy story about me being out of town and they needed to take care of my windows so they wouldn't be behind schedule. Apparently it took some convincing, but finally his boss gave in and told them to go ahead. I wasn't interested in dating at the time because the kids were still at home and I was working, so I already had a full life.

I ran into Ben every once in a while, or heard about him since we knew the same people. In 1997, I went to North Carolina to attend a funeral, and while I was there I ran into Ben. I found out he was living down there to take care of his mother. His sister knew I was in town and encouraged us to get together. I'm not sure whether it was because he reminded me of those simple times back in the projects, but I got a good feeling when I was around him. We connected as if no time had passed, although lots of things had changed for both of us. It felt nice enjoying the company of a good man like Ben. It was the first time since Emery passed that I felt maybe there was hope. Life does go on.

Dating wasn't a priority for me, but all of the children had their own lives, including Eric and Ellisha, and after the horrendous previous year I guess I was ready to let love in. The depression gradually receded into the crevices of my mind. It wasn't gone—there were still difficult moments where I would feel paralyzed by the truth of my reality—but things had improved. I had lost my father and my son, but I had so many other loving family members that I also started to get my appetite back and almost felt like a normal person again.

Ben was a welcome addition to my life and someone I could trust. He seemed to understand right away that I was broken, but mending, and he was patient. It felt good to have a new love in my life, a new feeling of excitement. I had butterflies, something I hadn't expected to feel again. Plus I knew that Ben liked my children, and they respected him, so it felt like a very natural transition.

Even today, a lot of people think he's Eric and Ellisha's father because he fit so naturally into the family, and he has always been very protective of them. He and Eric would occasionally get into disagreements, but they would always work it out and move on, like most families. I was grateful for the smooth transition since I didn't need any more disruptions in my family.

Ellisha had moved to Staten Island. She worked hard and did her best since leaving school to have her daughter. She had her son Mikey in 2006, ten years after Emery passed away. She moved back to Brooklyn and got married. I was proud of the way she had turned her life around. She took Mikey to daycare and ended up working there. The daycare director told her about free classes for food handlers, so she took classes, learned some skills, and worked in the kitchen for more than ten years. She said her motivation was her children, and she never forgot when Emery told her about getting her life on track.

In fact, Ellisha was so motivated that she surprised her daughter by getting her GED just before her daughter graduated from high school. She hadn't even realized that her momma hadn't graduated. Ellisha didn't stop there. While working as head cook at the daycare, she went to college and took up criminal justice, and just before graduation, the MTA contacted her about a job driving a bus. Without telling anyone, she took the driver's training class every morning in the Bronx, then went to school and work. She juggled her classes and graduated with a degree, and she got a job driving a bus. Some folks didn't understand why she was doing that instead of getting an office job, but the truth was she enjoyed it. I liked that she was with the MTA because that stability was good for her, just like it was for me.

After dating for a while after meeting up again in North Carolina, Ben and I had gotten married and were now living together, which felt nice since the children had moved out. Because we had known each other for a long time, things seemed to fall right in place. My children got along with him very well, and Ellisha called him Big Ben. He was very understanding when I would have my grandchildren over. I took care of Eric's children from day one and loved every minute of it. I was glad that Ben took it all in stride.

Eric had been living with his wife and four children over on Mother Gaston Boulevard in the Brownsville section of Brooklyn, not too far from me and Ben. Eric would bring the kids over to see us, and I'd go over there. I was always a surrogate mother for lots of children, so it felt very natural for me to have young kids around the house. I enjoyed being a grandmother to his kids and Ellisha's. At one point, Eric moved out of his home and stayed with me and Ben while he and his wife worked things out.

I loved having my son back home, despite the circumstances. Ben enjoyed having Eric around as well since he had recently retired from working construction. Eric wasn't working steadily at the time and did odd jobs or sold "loosies," usually on Bay Street in Staten Island. Selling individual cigarettes was not legal, but a lot of people (and even some stores) regularly did it as a way to make a few dollars. Plus, with the price of cigarettes, a lot of people couldn't afford to buy an entire pack.

Ben would occasionally go down to Bay Street and meet up with Eric and others who were regulars there. There are stores lined up on one side of the street and a small park on the other side. Most of the time, Ben, Eric, and the others would meet up in the park and play chess or checkers. Or they would walk along the street talking to store owners, employees, and customers whom they knew.

When Ben came home, he would tell me stories about the people over there and the things that happened. I was not surprised to find out that everyone loved it when Eric came around. He was a big teddy bear of a guy who always had a smile to share. Some were intimidated by him at first because of his size; he was 6 feet 3 inches and had grown to more than 350 pounds due to his medical issues and prescription drugs. But once he flashed that big smile, it broke the spell, and Eric would make a new friend.

Ramsey Orta was one of the guys who hung around the intersection of Victory Boulevard and Bay Street. He met Eric in the summer of 2009 when he was walking his dog, and they started hanging out the next year. I heard the story of how Ramsey's dog gave birth and Eric helped take care of the puppies so Ramsey could eventually sell them. Taisha Allen also lived in that area and was often shopping or hanging out. She became good friends with Eric and Ramsey, along with some of the other regulars. Taisha said that Eric was so friendly with everyone and always talking about his love for his family.

In New York, most people can't afford a large place to live, so they spend a lot of time outside. They find places they like and people they can relate to, and that's where they spend their days. From the sound of it, the people on Bay Street were like a family, and it reminded me of my neighborhood growing up. You had young men getting their hustle on, trying to make a few dollars; there were shop owners, clerks, even homeless folks down on their luck who hung out in the park. I heard plenty of stories about how when the ice cream truck lumbered down the street playing a tinny version of "Pop Goes the Weasel," Eric would flag the truck down and buy as much ice cream as he could afford and give it to the kids who gathered after school. They also occasionally had impromptu cookouts over at the park, and Eric would made sure all the homeless folks in the area were able to get some food in their bellies.

Stories like that didn't surprise me because I had seen that from Eric his entire life. I'm not saying he was perfect, but he always looked out for others, especially the underdogs. Any time he saw someone suffering or being mistreated, he just couldn't stand it. He had to help. To me, that was one of the most loveable qualities about him. Caring about other people and showing compassion can't be taught; it's part of your spirit. Booker T. Washington said that the best way to lift up oneself is to help someone else.

That was always Eric's mantra. The reason he was so kind to others and so protective of the weak was because it made him feel good to help. He didn't have a lot of money, but when he did have some he would not hesitate to share it. Even without money, he would give of himself. He would take the time to listen to someone and try to help solve a problem.

Over there on Bay Street they all looked out for each other, with Eric the caretaker, guys like Ramsey walking their dog or hanging out with their kids in the park, young women like Taisha visiting the convenience store or buying products at the discount beauty store, and retirees like Ben playing board games and talking about the good old days. They really enjoyed spending their days together, talking crazy and getting through the day. But there was a dark side.

Naturally, the Bay Street crowd felt protective of their turf and didn't like people coming around causing trouble or messing with their friends, no matter who they were. Everyone over there said that it was a regular occurrence for the police to show up and give folks a hard time. Whether it was breaking up a group of young Black men or questioning the homeless in the park, the police often made their presence known. Stories like that made me really nervous because I always thought back to Mr. King and those riots. I always told Eric to be careful, and Ben had done the same, especially since Eric had his share of police harassment.

The cops liked to use their knowledge of the locals to their advantage. If they knew something about someone's past, it would be used against them. There were no second chances. Since Eric had been in trouble for selling loosies, that was the go-to any time they wanted to stop him: "We know you are selling those cigarettes out here." It didn't matter if he was or he wasn't. If he denied it, if it wasn't true, they didn't care. They would use that as a form of control and intimidation. It frustrated Eric and the others because even if they were minding their own business, the police would come by and flex their authoritative muscle.

I certainly understood the need for police officers when it was warranted. If an actual crime was taking place or real trouble, that made sense to me. But we all got tired of dealing with the harassment and posturing on a daily basis. When you don't have as much as others, you are much easier to intimidate and control, and everyone knows that.

Eric got arrested one time, and he happened to have a bit of cash in his pocket. Ben went over to get him in downtown Brooklyn, but they had taken him to Riker's Island instead. Ben couldn't believe they had moved him so quickly, but he bonded Eric out and went with him to get his property. Eric realized that some of his money was missing and asked the attending officer where it was. He was told, "You're lucky you got that much back." Eric filed a police report about the missing money, even though I told him to just let it go. We all knew the police did not like that.

During the week of July 7, 2014, police officers made one of their surprise visits to Bay Street to make their presence known. When they saw Eric, one of them told him that if he would spend a week in jail, they would give him the rest of his money. Ben said that Eric told them he would do it if that's what it took to get his money back. Then, the next week, all hell broke loose.

The summer of 2014 was actually milder than usual. However, when you're in the city, the heat is magnified by the concrete sidewalks and dark asphalt. Even when the temperature isn't real high, it is still as hot and sticky as the thickest molasses. That relentless heat can drive folks crazy. It was during weather like that when I was glad that I worked underground most of the time.

On the morning of Thursday, July 17, I did a few chores and then reminded Ben to give my brother a ride to the hospital on Coney Island for his checkup. Before I got ready for work, I decided to call Eric because I hadn't heard from him in a couple of days. We always talked at least every other day, if not every day. I thought it was strange that recently when I had called it would go straight to voicemail. Finally, he answered at around 10:00 a.m.

"Eric, where have you been? I've been trying to call you for the last couple of days."

He said, "Oh, remember, Ma, I told you I was going to Baltimore to my wife's family reunion? For those two days we cut our phones off so we wouldn't have interruptions, but I thought it was OK since you knew where we were. We are home now."

"I totally forgot that you were going to Baltimore." We talked for a few minutes. Then I said, "Don't forget on Saturday it's our family reunion in Prospect Park."

He said, "I didn't forget. What do you need me to bring?"

"Just bring soda and water. We got the rest."

"OK, bye, Ma. I love you."

"Love you too."

I never dreamed that would be our last conversation, but instead of a family reunion on that Saturday, I was at a march in Staten

Island led by Reverend Al Sharpton to raise awareness about the murder of my son Eric.

I went on to work since I had to be there at 1:30 for my shift starting at 2:00 p.m. While I was driving one of the subway trains, a violent storm was brewing over on Bay Street. Eric was there reconnecting with his friends since he had been out of town for a few days. He met up with Ramsey, and they saw Taisha going into Bay Beauty Supply. As Eric and Ramsey were talking, they saw a fight break out, and naturally Eric went over to break it up. Because of his size, he usually just had to intervene, and they would immediately disperse.

Before that could happen, police officers pulled up, responding to a call by one of the local shopkeepers. They knew Eric, specifically because of the police report he had recently filed. They immediately went to him as the instigator and circled him in front of the beauty store like a caged animal. Ramsey pulled out his phone and began filming, despite being warned several times to stop.

Taisha did the same thing. She was inside the store and came out to explain what was going on. She told them Eric wasn't fighting; he was trying to break it up. She said they told her to mind her own business, but she's a tough woman. She said, "No, he's my friend and he was just breaking up the fight!" Realizing that they weren't going to stop, Taisha was going to call Internal Affairs to report the incident, but once she saw them push Eric to the ground, she knew there wasn't time for that.

She said she saw his eyes rolling back in his head as he gasped for breath as the chokehold tightened around his throat. She yelled, "You're choking him!" Once again, they told her to mind her own business. They often think people like Taisha can just be dismissed and written off, but that's not always the case. Sometimes folks can't take it anymore. Taisha had seen this scenario play out too many times, so she followed Ramsey's lead and used the only weapon she had—her cell phone.

Outside on the sidewalk, Ramsey was dealing with the same threats from the police as they told him to stop filming and to move along. Like Taisha, he refused, telling them he had a right to be there since he was not interfering. After all, if they were not doing anything wrong, why would they care that they were being filmed? What was the issue? In fact, they should have welcomed it, unless they had something else in mind.

After the horror of it all, after they wheeled my son to the ambulance, Taisha stayed and looked through the glass, watching as they sat for maybe twenty minutes without performing any kind of resuscitation. They finally drove off, returning later to string up yellow police tape since it was now a homicide investigation.

Ramsey, Taisha, and the other folks who had been in the beauty store and those watching on the sidewalk couldn't believe what had just happened in front of their eyes. Eric, their friend, had been harassed, then pinned on the ground until the life was choked out of him. Even as he yelled "I can't breathe!" they continued. How does that happen? Taisha even has the video of one of the officers smiling and waving at her as they left the scene. Next, the place was swarming with more police, news crews, and reporters. Ramsey and Taisha were interviewed on the news, and Ramsey shared his video with the *Daily News*.

Cynthia Davis, president of the Staten Island Office of the National Action Network (NAN), was in the neighborhood on another case when one of the witnesses ran up to her and told her what had just happened. She was reluctant to go investigate because she was headed to a different meeting, but the witnesses were insistent that she was needed. The police commander was in the taped-off section and raised the tape for her. They were acquainted because of the work she does to help families in need.

The commander explained to her that, as he understood it, a man was selling loose cigarettes on the street and resisted arrest. Since he was a large man, he must have had a heart attack during the arrest. When Cynthia spoke with the witnesses, however, they all presented basically the same story: No loosies. Breaking up a fight. Telling the police that he couldn't breathe. Still they persisted.

Cynthia even ran into a couple of caseworkers who had been with clients in the park. They all knew Eric from the neighborhood, and they corroborated the same story. She quickly realized that the "official" version didn't sound right.

Ben had taken my brother to the hospital like I asked him to. While they were there, a friend called Ben and said, "They are beating up your son over on Bay Street! They have him down on the ground!" Since Ben was all the way in Coney Island, he called my brother Larry and asked him to get over to Bay Street to see what was going on with Eric. It wasn't long before Larry called back and said, "Ben, Eric didn't make it." Ben was devastated. "No, don't tell me that. Do not tell me that!"

Ben couldn't believe what he had to do. It was up to him to come get me from work and break the news. He said it was the hardest thing he has ever done. When he came and picked me up from work that day, as soon as we got in the car I asked what was going on with Eric.

"Larry hasn't told me yet, Gwen. Let's go home." Then his phone rang. He answered it but didn't say anything after he hung up.

"Ben, was that Larry? What did he say?"

"He said he hasn't heard anything yet."

I knew that something was not right. "Ben, don't lie to me."

That's when he told me the news that shattered my world. I could not even make sense of it. He said that I tried to get out of the car, and I started kicking at the windows while we were on the parkway. He had to restrain me with one hand and drive with the other. He even tried to get the police to escort us to the hospital, but they didn't understand the urgency.

Ben called Ellisha as she was behind the wheel of the B-11 and told her the news. He'd left a message saying, "Ellisha, Eric is having trouble breathing." Once Ellisha got to the end of her route, she checked her voicemail and realized that something serious had happened. She called "Big Ben," as she referred to him. Ben told her, "It's not looking good." Ellisha didn't realize that Eric had been attacked. She thought his asthma was acting up again. She called her dispatcher and said, "I need to get to my family." Just about that time, Ben called her back with the news: "Eric didn't make it."

Once Ben pulled up to the home, I was a nervous wreck. I didn't know what to do with myself. I kept pacing the floor and saying his name over and over again. *Eric, Eric, Eric . . .* I was trying to process what had happened. I heard snippets about how the police had harassed my boy, how they put him in a chokehold, how they squeezed the breath right out of him in broad daylight. The more I thought about it, the sicker I felt. Didn't they know he had asthma? That he had trouble breathing? Had he told them that?

I could feel the devil wrap his strong hands of depression around my soul once again, one evil finger at a time. That familiar feeling was so warm and welcoming since it was something I knew all too well. I flashed back to when I lost Bernard and then almost twenty years later when Emery was taken from me. That depression had such a strong hold on me back then, and I could feel it coming back. At first I welcomed it—I embraced the feeling, allowed it into my heart and soul. I knew it would protect me from this pain and make it bearable. I would be swallowed in the dark abyss, but at least I would be able to cope with the horrible truth that my son was gone. Otherwise, how would I be able to survive?

With all of the news crews gathering in front of our house, we weren't sure what to do. Larry went out and got a reporter from the *Daily News*, who promised to print exactly what we told him. That's when we found out there was a video of the entire event. I knew I'd never be able to watch it. There was no way I could sit there as my son was tortured and abused right before my eyes. I could never put myself through that, and I still haven't. Plus, if I did see that, I'm not sure what I would have done because the fact remains that, like most mothers, I would die for my children if necessary, no questions asked.

All I could think about was when Eric was a little boy so concerned about making friends and sticking up for people. I thought about his friends always saying how cheerful and helpful he was, and how he looked out for others. I thought about him in home economics class, and later how he was with his own children. It didn't seem possible that my son was no longer alive. He was supposed to be at the reunion in two days. He was bringing the soda. He would be the life of the party, like always.

By Saturday, the day we had planned to get together with relatives in Prospect Park, the day we had planned to laugh and carry on while eating grilled food and playing games, we instead found ourselves down on Bay Street. Our family and members from Eric's family met Reverend Al Sharpton there so we could walk to the Staten Island police precinct in a show of solidarity against these crimes toward our people.

I couldn't look at the taped-off area in front of the beauty store. Imagining the horror that had occurred there was just too much for me. One thing I was thankful for was that I had asked Ben to carry my brother over to Coney Island Hospital that day. If he had been down on Bay Street when the tragedy went down, I know he would be in jail right now because he would have done anything to stop them from hurting our son.

As we gathered and waited for everyone to arrive, folks came out from all over to show their allegiance to the cause. Without saying a word, they all knew why we were there. It was a sad fact that we had all seen incidents like this before; it was an unfortunate part of our lives and one that unified us. As the crowd grew, some of the people there started to get worked up about the police brutality, and one guy threw a bottle. Ben stepped up and said, "Oh, hell no, we are not going to do that here. Not today. We are not going to tear up our own community. Not in Eric's name."

Lord knows I understood the pent-up anger and frustration that everyone was feeling, but there was a right way and a wrong way to express it. I did not want any violence going on, and Ben knew that. I don't think I could have made it through those dark days without him by my side. When I was weak, he was strong. He helped guide me through those difficult days with so much love and compassion that I fell in love with him all over again. I could just give him a look and he knew to take over, to handle things when I just couldn't.

When it was time to march, I held Reverend Sharpton's hand and the rest of the family formed a chain, interlocking our arms as we marched down the street, cars stopping along the way to show respect. I kept my jaws clenched and my fists tight. My stomach was tied up in knots as I realized the importance of what we were doing. Others fell in line behind us, and soon we were hundreds strong, all kinds of folks—Black, Brown, White—walking with one purpose.

Our faces were stern and our resolve absolute. We were there not just for Eric but also for everyone who felt disrespected and disenfranchised. Just because folks didn't have a lot of money or power didn't mean they were any less important. We walked for them.

I so appreciated Reverend Sharpton, Cynthia Davis, and the members of the National Action Network who had shown up to provide their support. They helped to mobilize us and bring attention to what we were doing, and I was grateful for that. I knew that as we marched down the street under the hot sun, the video that Ramsey had taken was playing endlessly on computers and cell phones all over the world. Now everyone could see what had happened to my boy with their own eyes.

Police brutality and harassment was no secret in our community. It was a part of everyday life for most non-Whites, especially for those who did not have a lot of money. They were weaker and easier to prey upon. With fewer financial resources and connections, the authorities knew their voices would likely never be heard. That's one of the reasons I was so grateful for a man like Reverend Sharpton, because he helped to give us the voice we so desperately needed.

Ramsey's video proved to be a game changer on many levels. Not since the Rodney King incident had such a brutal attack been recorded for the world to see. Finally, others could witness what we saw on a regular basis. Taisha's video also made its way into the ether, validating everything from a slightly different perspective.

As people viewed and shared the video many times over, everyone watched as they trapped my son like a caged animal. I have seen parts of it and heard what happened. Eric was so frustrated with the ongoing harassment, especially because he had done nothing wrong that day. Others even backed him up, trying to reason with the officers and help de-escalate the situation. It's true that he tried to avoid being handcuffed because he knew that once that happened, he would be totally helpless, once again at their authoritarian mercy.

He wasn't aggressive or assertive with those officers. He did what he always did—tried to calm everyone down and bring reason to the unreasonable, shed light in the darkness. He even asked them to please not touch him. He didn't struggle with them, just tried to use his words, but they were ignored. This is the part I have not watched, the part where they took him down with such force that he was slammed first into the storefront glass and then the sidewalk. Still he pled for mercy.

As the officers piled on him, one even pushed on his head with such force that he could not get air. His asthma was likely triggered by the stress of the situation and the way they blocked his airflow. It was just inhumane. I can't imagine a wild animal being treated in such a manner. The cries for mercy and the right to breathe just tear me up. Can anyone imagine if that was their child?

Apparently, it's obvious that there was something wrong because Eric didn't move after he was taken to the ground. He was in danger, but that was ignored. It just seems to me that common human decency would be to immediately get help, but that didn't happen. He was obviously in no condition to harm anyone, and still he was left to suffer. Every time I think about how he must have been feeling, my pulse quickens, and I start getting light-headed.

I can't explain the feeling of total helplessness that I continue to have. How could I not be able to protect my son? That was my job on this earth, and this was one time when I couldn't run to his aid. It wasn't like when he was an infant and I could *feel* that something was wrong with his breathing. He was an extension of me, and I knew then that he was suffering, that he wasn't breathing like the other children I'd seen at the hospital. He needed help, and I made sure he got it.

Out there on Bay Street, he did not get the same treatment. I was not able to save my son that time. His friends tried to intervene, but they were not able to get close enough to help. They all tried their best by filming and proclaiming his innocence, but the police kept them at bay. If they had felt there was no option but to arrest him, they should have done that without hurting him. It wasn't necessary. And when it was obvious that something was wrong, why didn't they get help? Isn't that a natural human instinct, to help someone when they need it? Weren't they sworn to protect and serve?

At least with the videos, the incident wouldn't get swept under the rug like so many others before it. There was now irrefutable evidence of the horrors that folks face out here every single day. Finally, the sheer terror and inhumaneness that poor folks have to deal with was captured with no edits, and no cuts. It was raw and real, the dirty truth of our world made public.

The one consolation was that with this evidence, things had to change. At least this would save other Black men and women from this inhumanity. With social media lit up by the incident, everyone on the planet would finally realize that people deserve human decency and fair treatment.

With every view and share of that evidence, things had to improve. Others would be saved from this travesty because law enforcement would be more cautious from now on. With cell phones pointed at them recording every moment, it meant that things had to get better; they just had to. I was sure that once people saw what happened, Eric's death would be vindicated, and the officers would pay dearly for what they had done to my boy.

I was sure of it.

# Chapter 4

## The Chokehold

One day our descendants will think it incredible that we paid so much attention to things like the amount of melanin in our skin or the shape of our eyes or our gender instead of the unique identities of each of us as complex human beings.

—Franklin Thomas

BEN KNEW RAMSEY FROM BEING OVER on Bay Street. Ben said that he often talked to Eric, Ramsey, and some of the other guys about being careful and staying out of any potential problems by just minding their own business. If Eric was the easygoing one, Ramsey was a little more cautious and closed off. He had been through a lot in his young life, and it seemed to weigh on him, to wear him down, but he was still out there doing what he had to do.

After we found out from the *Daily News* reporter about the video, Ben asked where they had gotten it, and they told him that Ramsey Orta had given it to them. With the reporter's help, they were able to locate Ramsey and bring him over to the house so that we could meet. I was still shell shocked from everything that happened when I saw the thin, young man standing there in my living room.

We stared at each other like deer in headlights, stunned by our shared grief, neither of us knowing what to say. I had just lost my son, and he had witnessed the brutality of his friend being choked to death. We were connected by that horrible moment and were both still processing it. I looked into his eyes and could see the concern and compassion he felt for Eric. Meeting him was an important moment, but I also regretted it for a second because it was another piece of the puzzle, more confirmation that this was not some horrible dream. Talking to Ramsey made me realize that my son was never coming back. This was real.

Fortunately, Ben was there to break the spell and help bridge the silence. Ramsey looked down at the floor a lot as he told us bits and pieces about what had happened. He didn't focus on that too much. Instead, he began sharing stories with us about Eric's generosity and how he took care of everyone, how he was always on the lookout for others. He said Eric was well respected, and he was very fatherly to a lot of the young folks over in the Bay Street neighborhood. I liked hearing that because I could picture him giving advice and trying to help others. He was always like that. He had plenty going on in his own life, but that never stopped him from trying to help other people, especially those who seemed troubled and lonely. Ramsey said that it was an honor to meet me because I was the mother Eric had talked so much about.

I wasn't able to say a lot except "thank you." I must have said it one hundred times, like I was on repeat. I was just so grateful that he had been brave enough to stand up for his friend despite the chaos that was happening in front of him. It took a lot of courage to do that, and I wanted him to know we were eternally grateful. He was put in a horrible situation, and he could have just run out on his friend, but he didn't. That made him very special in my eyes.

Ben asked Ramsey to come to Eric's funeral service, but he said that he would rather not. Maybe it was too painful for him, too raw. I certainly understood that and didn't want to push him, but I did say that he would be welcome to come to the funeral or to our home if he ever needed to. As far as I was concerned, he was now part of the family.

I was not looking forward to Wednesday, July 23, 2014. That was the date for Eric's service, and I dreaded it. This would give finality to everything, that my son was gone forever. The last few days had been a whirlwind of grief and gratitude. While Eric and I had a close relationship, I wasn't with him every day, and he had his own life. As people started approaching me with stories about him, I learned so much that it was almost like a reawakening, a reaffirmation of the good qualities my son possessed. I knew it all along, but it felt good that so many other people felt the same way about him.

My picture had been plastered all over the news after Eric was killed. Not only photos but also video of interviews and publicity from the march in Staten Island with Reverend Al Sharpton and the NAN people. There was so much media after everything happened that I wasn't sure what was going on. The activity swirled around me like a windstorm. It was very unnerving at first, since I've always been a private person. I've never been one who enjoyed being the center of attention. That was more of Eric's personality or Emery's, but not me. I'd always been quieter, reserved. My parents had taught me to behave in a certain way, and that's what I'd always done. Now things were different. I was in the public eye, and I didn't have much choice about it.

Everywhere I went, people would come up to me—slowly at first, hesitant, asking whether I was Eric's mother. Once I confirmed their suspicion, they would invariably launch into a story about how he had helped them or how he reminded them of their son or brother or husband. I did love hearing those stories. Eric livened up every family event he attended, so I knew the effect he had on people. However, it was heartwarming to hear from so many strangers that he was important to them, too. I had no idea he knew so many folks, of all types and age ranges.

He was just always like that. He connected with everyone, and there was no hesitation on his part. Despite his faults, I was very proud of the fact that he was always so willing to give of himself, that it came so naturally for him. I wouldn't have been more impressed if he had been rich and famous. Being kind and generous are traits that are much more important to me than any material things could ever be.

Still, I found it difficult getting used to being recognized. I got a little paranoid because I always felt like I was being watched, which I was! I could see the stares and the quick glances, hear the low whispers. Don't get me wrong, it was all done respectfully for the most part, but it was unnerving and still is. I'd gone from the anonymity that I loved to being recognized everywhere I went. I could tell when someone connected the dots and realized who I was. It would register on their face the second they placed in their mind that I was the mother in the countless news stories that blanketed the media, especially around the city.

It usually didn't take more than five or ten seconds, but I learned to treasure that precious time before the questions began. For that brief moment, it felt like things were back to the way they were before. I was just a wife, mother, and MTA worker minding my own business and enjoying my smoggy city life. Once I was recognized, reality would come back like a sledgehammer. I was reminded of everything that happened, and each time it felt as raw and painful as the first. I didn't like being forced to think about it again. I enjoyed those rare moments when I could conjure up other thoughts that would provide temporary relief from my reality.

With every interaction, I tried to put on a brave face, tried to remain stoic. I loved their stories, I really did, but the pain that accompanied them was torture. Getting used to not having Eric around felt unnatural, like a cruel joke. For a long time, I didn't realize that I was still referring to him in the present tense. I would say things like "Yes, he's a wonderful man" or "He is always doing things like that." Sometimes I'd get a confused look, but most people were very understanding.

Sometimes I'd get introduced as Eric Garner's mother, and then they would explain to the other person who he was and what had happened. That got to be very uncomfortable for me. I know they were just trying to give some context to the situation, but I did not need to hear the story over again. I had lived it. I *was* living it. I will always live it. That didn't happen all the time, but it was more than I would have liked.

In our large, extended family, I had always been a surrogate mother to many of the children—nieces, nephews, cousins. It was just natural for me to take on a caregiver role with all the little ones. So it was interesting when the entire city saw me as "the mother" of Eric Garner. I was seen first as a mother and then as Gwen Carr, the person. To some that might seem odd, but to me it felt right, and I began to understand the power of that title. That's where I've always felt comfortable, so to get that recognition locally, nationally, and then globally just reinforced the path I'd chosen in this world. Being seen as a good parent is the highest of honors, in my opinion.

My son's funeral was held at Bethel Baptist Church, located on Bergen Street in the Boerum Hill area of Brooklyn. The church was built almost one hundred years ago and is a beautiful brick building. I wasn't focused too much on the details, though, because it was a frenzy of activity. Reverend Al Sharpton and his National Action Network paid for the service and handled most of the logistics. It was a relief to know that they were managing everything and making sure the details were taken care of.

Our family was there in full force, taking up the first floor. There were folks from the Garner side and from the Flagg side. There were some from Davis and Jones—it was amazing to see so much support. That's one thing about our large family: We have plenty of internal drama going on, like most folks, but we all pull together when times are tough. Having some of our people up from North Carolina and seeing a sea of coordinated T-shirts to identify family members made me feel better under the difficult circumstances.

The service felt different from others I've attended, mostly because of the obvious police presence outside. The atmosphere was a bit tense because of how Eric had been killed, and seeing those uniformed officers outside of my son's service made me feel some type of way. I understood they wanted to make sure things didn't get out of control, but I didn't like the reminder of how my son had died standing right outside the door. It was a different story inside. There were so many people that they had to lock the doors to stop anyone else from entering. I had no idea there would be so many people, or I would have tried to get them to find an even larger facility. The families of two other victims of police-involved incidents, Amadou Diallo and Sean Bell, were there to show support.

Local advocates spoke out with initiatives, including suggesting that police need to video record all future encounters to help prevent this from happening again. Because the city had been so affected by the incident, everyone noticed the glaring absence of Mayor Bill de Blasio. Like so many politicians, he had been quick to denounce the brutality and promise a full investigation, but instead of showing up at my son's funeral, he was off on a fancy trip with his own son while I was burying mine. To me, that wasn't right. As mayor, when something horrible happens in your city, you change your plans and show up. That's my opinion.

Despite that, the service was a moving tribute to everything Eric stood for. Reverend Al did his thing up there onstage, celebrating Eric and chastising the sheer brutality of the situation. That's when he said, "You don't need no training to stop choking a man saying, 'I can't breathe.'" I was pleasantly surprised when Mr. Sharpton brought Ramsey up onstage. He had been able to make it after all, and I was so glad that he did. I was told he'd been given some money to buy a suit, and I thought he looked very nice. In front of everyone, he was celebrated for standing up for justice and not running from the situation. I know that people say Al Sharpton has his faults, but the fact that he made sure Ramsey got there was wonderful. I was happy that the young man was getting the recognition because he deserved it. I gave him a big hug later and thanked him, once again, for all he had done.

Ellisha sang a beautiful song at the service, and many others spoke about how Eric had positively influenced their lives. It was amazing to see so many people, many who hadn't even actually met my son, who came to show solidarity because this had happened in their community, on their street. It affected all of us and reminded us that we were tired of the way we have always been treated. As Reverend Sharpton said onstage when they talked about providing more police training, "You don't need no training to stop choking a man saying, 'I can't breathe.'"

I watched most of the ceremony through tears as I kept getting reminded about how important Eric was to all of us. It was a hot summer night, and, with so many people packed inside, it was very warm, but I didn't let that bother me. As I looked out over the rows of people, I watched the paper fans flutter like beautiful white doves mourning the tragic loss of such a beautiful life. I could hear some of the protesters outside shouting for justice. I understood their mission and the frustration they were feeling, so that didn't bother me, either. They were very respectful and grew silent when the casket was carried outside and into the awaiting car.

Eric was dressed in a turquoise shirt and a white suit. There were beautiful flowers and an inscription that read "Beloved Brother." I saw the terrible pain that his family was going through, and it tore me up. He had left behind his wife and children. We were all suffering, and there was no relief in sight. We each had to find our own way to deal with the heartache of loss.

While we were mourning the loss of Eric, changes were slowly taking place at city hall. Police officer Daniel Pantaleo, the man who had choked my son to death, was placed on "modified assignment" during the internal investigation that was supposed to be happening. However, he was still able to keep his badge, which didn't seem right to me. The EMS workers who showed up at the scene and failed to perform emergency measures were suspended from work without pay.

William Bratton, the NYPD commissioner, said officers would be "retrained" on how to respond to calls. A lot of this trouble started because of what is referred to as "quality of life" patrols, in which officers routinely harass citizens with low-level offenses. This comes from what is called the "broken windows" strategy, which basically means heavily policing folks who are usually not actually breaking the law but have been known to be in trouble in the past. The line of thinking is that this type of policing will prevent further escalation, but that has never been proven. I did my research and found out that there has been no hard, irrefutable evidence that this method does anything other than harass and further exacerbate a nonviolent situation.

To me, this is yet another tactic that is used to mask the intimidation of poor Black folks by saying that it's for the good of the community and that the residents and shop owners have asked for it. Eric was a frequent target of this "policy," and that's why in the video he kept saying they were always harassing him and he was tired of it. Can you imagine being accused of something you didn't do and how frustrating that would be? Can you imagine being constantly confronted by the very people who are supposed to be protecting you? The NYPD doesn't just work for the well-to-do; the police are supposed to be there for everyone. Eric deserved just as much respect as anyone else in the city, but, as we could all see in the video, he was treated like he didn't matter, and like what he said meant nothing.

I think the most effective way to improve police effectiveness is through training, but not the usual "feel good" approaches that are typically implemented to appease angry citizens. The best way is to provide instruction on ways the police can build trust at the local level, in the communities, like neighborhood watch programs. When a community feels more engaged in policing their homes, they can work together to protect the entire neighborhood. When law enforcement officers work closely with the residents, they are much more likely to create a collaborative atmosphere of safety and security. Targeting specific citizens, and almost always Black males, and constantly harassing them under the guise that it will ultimately protect the community seems ineffective and cruel to me.

On Bay Street, just like in hundreds of neighborhoods across the city (and the country, for that matter), folks usually take it upon themselves to look out for each other. Thanks to those "broken windows" tactics, they have lost trust in police officers. Establishing two-way communication and building relationships with the people is how law enforcement could truly improve their image after all of the brutality cases; instead, they choose just the opposite.

Outreach and engagement programs that start with young people seem like they would be much more effective than harassing people just because they think it will prevent something worse from happening one day in the future. Working with the homeless population and engaging folks who are in the streets every day would give officers a better view of what is happening out there, and it would help others realize the police intentions are there to help, not to harass.

We are so socially aware and connected these days with cell phones and social media. The old tactics of brute force are no longer viable. We can see everything now. We teach our children how harmful and destructive bullying is, but then they see the exact same behavior from those who are paid by our tax dollars to protect us. It doesn't make sense.

It would be much more effective to use those modern-day tools to their advantage, to create more outreach and immediacy with the people out in the community day in and day out. Police presence does not have to equate to intimidation. Learning how to be a part of the community would be a valuable way to build trust, instill pride, and show common human decency to those who need it the most.

I know there are no simple answers, but I do think change is possible. I always taught my children to respect law enforcement and to watch how they come across. Even after everything that has happened, I certainly don't blame all officers for Eric's death—just the opposite. I only want to see justice against those who actually participated in my son's suffering and choking. They are the only ones at fault in my opinion.

The medical examiner declared Eric's death a homicide and said that he died as the result of a chokehold. The report said my son died due to "compression of chest and prone positioning during physical restraint by police," according to the medical examiner spokesperson. It has never been released—yet another mystery. We all knew that to be true because everyone saw it on the video, but it was satisfying to hear an expert announce it to the world. I thought that meant we would actually see justice served. The medical examiner said that the way Eric was restrained on the ground compressed his neck and chest. That harsh treatment, along with his asthma and weight, contributed to his death.

Then things started to go left. Patrick Lynch, the president of the Patrolmen's Benevolent Association of New York, made a statement that the autopsy report was "political," whatever that means, and also asserted that there was no chokehold. He also had the audacity to say that the way people are treated by the police has nothing to do with who they are or how they look. Unless you are a part of a minority or the disenfranchised and have walked in their shoes, you don't know how they are treated. You might like to think everyone is treated fairly, but I can promise you that's just not the case. We all make judgments based on appearance. That's a fact of life. To say otherwise is just not true.

About a month after Eric was killed, the NYPD announced that it was conducting an investigation into the incident with the help of district attorneys and detectives. When it was announced that the case would go to the grand jury, we again had hope that we would get answers and that justice would be served.

As the investigation began to snake through the legal system, I was in the nail salon when a young lady came up to me. By now I was used to people approaching me from out of nowhere. Almost all of them were sympathetic and gracious, so I had grown accustomed to it.

"Hi, are you Mrs. Carr?" she asked.

"Yes, I am."

"I'm Taisha. I was there that day."

That's all she had to say. "That day" had become shorthand for the day when my son was killed, choked to death. Calling it "that day" was a way for us to talk around it. We didn't have to bring up the horrible details, except this time we did.

"I saw you when you came to Bay Street with Al Sharpton. I've also talked to your daughter, Ellisha. I took a video that day with my phone," she told me. "I was in the beauty store when it happened. Ramsey and I were both filming, even though the cops tried to stop us."

Ellisha had told me someone talked to her about another video, which didn't surprise me since there had been a lot of people coming and going on "that day." I didn't focus on it too much at the time, because I never plan to watch the original video, much less another one, but the young lady seemed so sincere.

"Eric was so nice to everyone in the community," she told me. "He was a big teddy bear. He would help anyone and everyone. He even helped a lady get off the drugs that were messing her up. He was very respected over there on Bay Street and at the park. He was a protector."

I got a little misty eyed hearing that because it made me so proud of him, but it also made me realize just how much I missed

him. I used to look forward to our chats on the phone and him drop-
ping by to visit me when I got off work. The simple fact was that I
missed my boy.

"Don't worry, Mrs. Carr, just be strong," Taisha said. "I'm going
to share the video and try to be a voice for the community."

I thanked her for the kind words. Having the neighborhood,
people I didn't even know, come together like that really made me
feel good. Plus, I liked the fact that they were doing things in Eric's
name. They were honoring him. He deserved that.

In the months that followed, I found out that things got difficult for Ramsey and Taisha. After that video went viral, Ramsey
was known the world over, and not just by supporters but also by
law enforcement. He started having a lot more run-ins with police
after that incident, and that makes it seem like he has been targeted
because he captured them in the act of brutalizing Eric. He said
officers would allude to him being the one who made that video.

Ramsey's home was raided in 2015, and he was arrested on a
drug charge that resulted in him taking a plea deal. Even though he
felt it wasn't justified, he decided to do his time and then get out. He
has received even worse treatment since he has been incarcerated,
including being denied visitors and put in solitary confinement. He's
been moved from one facility to another, which has made access for
his family and friends even more difficult, which certainly wasn't
coincidental, no matter what they say.

Even in jail he has been subjected to harsh treatment just because of who he is and what he did, which in my opinion was one of
the bravest things anyone could have done. To me, he is a hero, and
I told him that myself. Once right after I first met him, when they
hauled him into jail on some trumped-up charge, I went down and
signed for him because I felt I owed him that much.

He never asked for any of this. He never wanted to be "famous."
He was just trying to help his friend. I can't imagine what it must
have been like for him to watch that play out on the sidewalk right
in front of him. Seeing the video (at least the parts I've seen) is horrible, so to actually have been there must have just been frightening.
It's just very frustrating for all of us when Brown and Black folks are

treated with such cruelty. Handling police business is one thing, but to actually target, torture, and abuse someone merely because he didn't back down is just wrong.

I would think that while the police didn't like that it was one of their own in the spotlight, they would be supportive of someone who got involved and stood up for his beliefs. Too often the police complain that no one will cooperate, or no one will come forward. Well, Ramsey did come forward and he did speak up for the truth, and so did Taisha. That is exactly what I was talking about with police needing to learn how to develop trust and respect in the community.

For this book, I contacted Ramsey in prison and asked him what message about Eric he would share with others. He wrote:

> I feel a lot more could have been done on all of our behalfs after his death which is why when I come home I will continue to seek and fight justice in his name.
>
> Looking back on everything now and where I am at today just makes me stronger for my future. The feelings I have built up inside of me towards NYPD is of hate and resistance. Yet, it has given me the power to stand on both feet and fight, rather than to kneel and show weakness! Long live Eric Garner!

All I can say is that I wish more people had just half of Ramsey's conviction. I'm serious about that. Look at all that has happened to him just because he tried to help. To me, the police should be glad when others are filming them because then they can prove that they are following protocol and acting appropriately . . . unless, of course, they aren't.

It might be easy to just write Ramsey off and say that he was only arrested by the police because he had broken the law. However, the exact same treatment has happened to Taisha after she refused to stop recording "that day." Since my son was killed, she has been harassed countless times. She said they would say things to her like "Oh, you are that b**** that filmed the Eric Garner video." Whenever they realized who she was, she would face harassment, and she said she was even attacked. She said that she has been thrown to the ground, beaten with a baton, and dragged by her feet. Like Ramsey, she felt she had to take a plea to get out from under their grip, but it has not stopped. Her harassment continues to this day.

I find it hard to believe that any type of new training program has been implemented within the department because this kind of thing happens so often. The one thing that I always say, though, is that not every police officer is like that. Most of them, in fact, try to do the right thing and treat folks with respect. It's those few who go too far, who don't follow procedure, that give them a bad name, and those are the ones who I think should be reprimanded. If internal programs were implemented to properly handle those rogue offi-cers, it would show that overall they are dedicated to truly serving the community with fairness and integrity.

One of the good things that came out of "that day" was that the NYPD reportedly re-evaluated its policy on chokeholds. Apparently, each department was using a different definition of what a choke-hold is and is not. Of course, that could all be cleared up by using proper training so that everyone knows what they can and cannot do. And the reason they cannot use that technique is because it can kill! It's literally a matter of life and death.

Despite the closure that a funeral is supposed to provide, I still could not believe that I had lost another son to violence, especially when I have always preached peace and civility. I brought two boys into this world, and now I was left with none. I had outlived both of them, and that is something no mother should have to endure, much less to go through twice in one lifetime.

My days are a roller coaster of emotions. Some days I'm able to convince myself that I'm OK, that things are fine, and that I have my emotions under control. The next day everything feels dark and sad, like a rain cloud that won't go away. I keep searching for the sunlight, for a glimpse of the strong rays that will burn away the darkness, but some days it does not come.

Nights are even worse. At first, I welcomed the darkness be-cause I thought when I fell asleep that's where I could escape the reality of what had happened. In dreamland, anything is possible. However, what I found is that when the lights go out, that's when the devil gets very comfortable. Instead of slowing down my mind and slipping into a sweet slumber, my thoughts speed up, swirling around in a dervish and reminding me of everything that happened.

I realize that no matter how bad I might feel, it's the daytime that offers some relief. That's when I can spend time with family and friends, when I can busy myself with other tasks to keep my mind occupied. At night, I'm helpless. My thoughts take over, and I keep wondering what I could have done differently or how I could have stopped this from happening to my family. I keep searching for something that I know I will never find. I keep searching for answers.

As odd as it may sound, the one thing that has helped me is the small shrine I have created for Eric in my living room. There is an empty chest that once held gifts of fruits and candies. Now I store some of his things in it—his old toothbrush, some medicine. I also have a group of photos that remind me of happier times. They are in old, tarnished frames, but I'm afraid to change them because they may rip or tear in the process. I don't think I could bear losing those images of my first son.

Some people think I've gone overboard with all my photos, and maybe I have, but I don't care. I'm not taking them down any time soon. I also have Christmas stockings—not just for Eric, Emery, and Ellisha but also for all my grandchildren and great-grandchildren.

I leave them up all year round. It's the least I can do.

# Chapter 5

---○---

# Rallying Cry

We all have dreams. In order to make dreams come into reality, it takes an awful lot of determination, dedication, self-discipline and effort.

—Jesse Owens, world-record-setting Olympic athlete

On Monday, September 29, 2014, the New York grand jury hearing began and lasted for two months. The purpose of the jury was to determine whether police officer Pantaleo would face charges for choking my son. It was reported that the other officers at the scene received immunity in exchange for their testimony, but since the hearing was private, no one really knows what was said or done. Pantaleo was the one at the center of the investigation. There were twenty-three members of the jury, and it was racially mixed, with fourteen White and the others Brown and Black.

During the time between my son's death and the grand jury, another tragedy had befallen our country. In August 2014, Michael Brown, another Black man, was killed by a White police officer, and that ignited the riots in Ferguson, Missouri. That tension spilled over into cities across the nation, including the already edgy residents of Staten Island. I could not believe that after Eric's death, it was still happening. There was no end in sight. I felt frustrated and helpless.

As far as the grand jury went, we all thought that the medical examiner's report and the videos shot by Ramsey and Taisha should have been all the evidence necessary for an indictment. How could anyone deny that? Whenever I was interviewed, I kept stressing to everyone that regardless of the ruling, there should be no violence in the community. We could figure out a way to get our message out in a peaceful manner. I just hoped people were listening, because with all that had happened I wasn't feeling very confident in folks staying peaceful. They were justifiably angry.

Sure enough, despite all the evidence and testimonies from Ramsey, Taisha, the beauty supply store owner, and many others, the grand jury returned with the decision not to indict NYPD officer Daniel Pantaleo. I was devastated by the news, but I wasn't surprised. I began to realize that this kind of constant disregard for minority folks was nothing new. Some family members were very angry by the ruling, and I understood that. Reverend Sharpton put it best when he said that this type of incident was a national crisis.

After that ruling, our only hope was for the case to be reviewed by the U.S. Department of Justice. At that time, Eric Holder was the U.S. attorney general, and he made a statement that there would be an investigation into Eric's death, including a review of all of the material and testimony already collected. Unfortunately, that information remains sealed from the public "to protect witness identity." At least that's what officials have told us.

As further encouragement, President Obama met with Mayor de Blasio and Al Sharpton at the White House in the fall of 2014 to discuss not only the unrest that was happening in Ferguson but also the next step in the investigation of my son's death. It seemed that Obama had the same idea that I did—to build trust and accountability with law enforcement and the communities they served.

That same month of the ruling, Eric's immediate family had sued the city and was eventually awarded a sum of $5.9 million to be divided among his wife, children, and grandchildren. That also included the baby that he just found out he had a couple of months before he passed away.

Eric had moved out of his home and stayed with me and Ben for a few months. During that time, he met a woman named Jewel and often stayed with her. He helped with her children, and she helped him with his health by encouraging better habits. She made sure he took his steroid medication, despite the fact that it made him gain weight. To counteract that, she also got him eating better and getting more exercise. In fact, when he first started gaining weight, I would ask him, "Eric, where are you getting this weight from?" He had always been a skinny kid, but the medication had an effect on him. However, by changing some of his habits, his asthma had even improved.

I tried hard to stay out of my son's personal business because I didn't want to get in the middle of anything. All I wanted to do was celebrate my grandchildren and be a mother, grandmother, and even great-grandmother. So I let him go through personal issues on his own. All I could do was support my son's choices and encourage him to do what made him happiest. I was excited to find out about Legacy, my newest grandchild, because I love babies and because she was a part of my son. She was premature, so she was already struggling in her young life, but when I first saw her I knew that she was Eric's daughter. I just knew it.

Now, I'll be honest and say that not everyone liked that there was a new baby, and from a woman who was not his wife, but I felt like I had to celebrate all of my grandchildren. That's what a grand-mother is supposed to do. I didn't like the tension it caused, but this little girl had nothing to do with that. She just wanted and needed love, especially after her father was gone. I cannot even begin to imagine what it will be like for her to grow up and eventually com-prehend what happened to her father. Of course, she will see the video at some point as well. My heart hurts just thinking about that. I also want to make sure she is involved with our family, with Eric's extended family, since that will always be part of her heritage.

When there were family functions, Eric would bring his children and sometimes their siblings, even though he wasn't their father. I guess it was a little complicated, but that was always his nature. He wanted to include everyone and just loved it when people got along. That was really when he was happiest as far as I'm concerned.

Unfortunately, I did have some previous experience with the New York justice system. On the morning of October 27, 2013, just nine months before Eric's death, my nephew Joseph Flagg III (Lil Joe) was murdered at the restaurant/candy store he owned. Fortunately, they caught the killers, three young men all under the age of eighteen. I joined his wife, Zakiyyah, her brother, her children Brooke and Nia, and her friend Bridgette as we sat in the courtroom month after stressful month waiting for a decision. We listened as one of the defendants attempted to portray himself as the victim, but after reviewing all of the evidence, two of them took a plea and received a ten- and a fifteen-year sentence. The other one went to trial and eventually received a thirty-year sentence in April 2017, about three and a half years after the tragedy.

I read somewhere that one of the best ways to combat depression is to get involved in new activities. I had been severely despondent when my first husband died, and even more so when my son Emery was killed. I already knew some of the warning signs—feelings of hopelessness, loss of appetite, sleep issues, no energy, anger, and recklessness. I knew them all, and I'd succumbed to all of them too.

Previously I had lost lots of weight because I just didn't care. It wasn't because I didn't want to care . . . I just couldn't. I was not *able* to care. It was the strangest feeling to suddenly be overtaken by such a heavy sense of nothingness. I was so used to doing things like looking after the children, running a household, working a full-time job—and then all of a sudden it was like that was flushed away. It didn't matter anymore. I wanted to care, I wanted to fix dinners and visit with family, but it felt like I was weighed down. It was such a different feeling for me, and everyone was alarmed because they knew how busy and active I usually was. Eric and Ellisha were especially concerned, particularly after Emery's death, when they were old enough to understand the magnitude of the situation. They did their best to bring me out of it.

It felt good to have people so concerned about me, but that still wasn't enough. Growing up, we never focused much on feeling sad or "depressed" or being overly emotional. We were too preoccupied with trying to earn a living and have a decent life. We didn't really have time to talk about feelings and emotions. So, it felt odd that my life had come to a screeching halt because of how I was feeling, but it was real and it was powerful. That oppressive feeling was like nothing I'd ever felt before, and something I'd never wish on anyone.

Because it is invisible, it's not like an obvious injury or physical condition, and that means some folks don't have a good understanding of it. I know I didn't until it happened to me. It all takes place in the recesses of your brain. It takes your soul hostage and invades your whole being. That makes it difficult for others to understand what you are going through. Yes, they know that there's been a tragedy and that it's normal to feel sad, but this goes way beyond that. So when the sadness lingers on long past when others think it should have subsided, their compassion begins to slowly fade and is replaced with frustration. That comes from not being able to comprehend just how difficult it can be to break out of that dark grip of the devil.

My family was especially concerned and caring, but I sensed that even they were getting tired of seeing me tired. I definitely didn't blame them. It was hard for me to understand what was happening, so I know it was not easy for others. Just the fact that they hung in there with me and helped where they could meant the world to me, and it still does. As that fog finally, ultimately loosened its grip on my soul, that's when I really started to comprehend all they had been doing for me. Before that, I was just so busy fighting to get back to my true self, and that took all of my energy.

I think the inability to fall asleep was a large part of it because I'd been scared to close my eyes, so I'd be up all night and then exhausted the next day. It was very unhealthy, but it was a cycle that I had such a hard time breaking out of. The evil spirit of depression had a real strong grip on me, and he was not about to let go. That was not a pleasant time in my life, and after Eric's murder I knew that I had to approach things differently.

At first, I fell back into those old ways. I was despondent, didn't want to talk to anyone, didn't want anyone to come over, didn't want to go anywhere. It was so much easier to retreat inside and hide away from the evils of the world. That is exactly what had happened before when I experienced tragedy. I just wanted to retreat from the world. Maybe that comes from being raised to keep things in the family and to take care of our problems ourselves. We weren't much for seeking help when it came to family issues. We either resolved them ourselves or just moved on, hoping they would fade into the crevices.

However, I did realize that just because that was the easy way, I couldn't go back there. I could not allow that evil to grab hold of me again. It was just too unhealthy, and my family was concerned that I might once again fall back into that dangerous pattern. Ellisha was especially worried since she had seen it before and knew the impact it could have not just on me but also on everyone around me.

With Eric's death, that was much different because it was so public. I did not have the cloak of anonymity that I had had before. This time, it was all out in the public. All of our family business was out there for the world to see and discuss and judge. That meant not only the positive aspects, such as the focus on police brutality and living as a Black person in an often racially charged environment, but also the negatives out there.

People who watched the video made judgments not only about the law enforcement and their actions but also about my son. Because of the way he was dressed and the location where everything took place, it was easy for folks to come to their own conclusions about his life. It was difficult to get used to everything being so public like that. Because of those viral videos, there was no escaping those images, the comments, the blogs and tweets, and on and on.

All of that attention was a lot to take, and it wasn't just affecting me but the whole family as well. It was also interesting to see how it impacted different relatives. It pulled some of us closer together, but it also drove others away. It's hard to understand, but that kind of horrific tragedy affects people differently, and you just never know how someone will react until they are faced with it.

I just let them all be and hoped they would come to terms with things in their own way. In the meantime, I had to make sure that I was healthy. That meant keeping those damn demons away and trying to move forward. That's one thing that I was learning through my life journey. No matter what challenges are thrown my way, no matter what I come up against in my life, I have to figure out a way to process it, deal with it, and keep moving forward. If I don't, it's all over for me. I can't allow myself to spiral downward like that. I have to keep on living and figure out the best way to do that.

Cynthia Davis was on Bay Street on "that day." It's part of her job. As president of the Staten Island branch of the National Action Network, she's a community outreach advocate. She works closely with law enforcement and the folks in the community, almost like a liaison to try to bridge the gap between the authorities and the people on the street. On "that day" two of the local residents had run up to her and told her about Eric being harassed down the street. She was on her way to another appointment and begged off, telling them she was already late for a meeting, but they were insistent. They told her she needed to go see what was going on, so that's what she did.

The cops allowed her under the yellow tape since they worked with her often, and she remained there for about forty-five minutes as the investigation went on. She immediately asked the commander what happened and was told that there was a man selling cigarettes who had resisted arrest. He was overweight and was taken to the hospital, where he appeared to have died of a heart attack.

Unfortunately, Cynthia had seen this type of situation many times before and didn't think the explanation sounded right. She and some of the other National Action Network people she worked closely with were often in that neighborhood, sometimes over in Tompkinsville Park, across the street from the crime scene, where they tended to the homeless and tried to help others who were struggling.

As president of the local National Action Network (NAN) office, Cynthia Davis was consulted on anything that seemed amiss in the area, and the scene on the sidewalk in front of the beauty supply store was certainly out of the ordinary. Cynthia sprang into action and interviewed a lot of the local witnesses, asking them what they had seen. She found out that their stories lined up almost exactly with each other, but that sounded nothing like what the police had told her.

Then she talked to the caseworkers who were in the area. They corroborated the story. They knew Eric from the neighborhood and couldn't believe that he was accused of resisting arrest. They had seen that he, like others in the area, was routinely harassed by the police, just to keep everyone on edge. They had seen him dealing with this type of situation before, and with his easygoing demeanor they knew that he would not harm anyone, especially the cops. He just wouldn't do it.

So, when Al Sharpton and his group, NAN, arranged for a march the day after Eric was murdered (and another one over the week), I met Cynthia and was immediately impressed by her passion and drive for working to bring about positive change. Of course, I knew who Al Sharpton was, and I'd heard of the National Action Network, but I never really thought much about what it did. I knew it was something about working with the community, but I just never focused on it too much. Cynthia invited me to come to its Saturday morning meeting, so I did some research on the organization.

The website caught my attention right away with the headline "No Justice, No Peace." Then I read the description: "The National Action Network is one of the leading civil rights organizations in the Nation, with chapters throughout the entire United States. Founded in 1991 by Reverend Al Sharpton, NAN works within the spirit and tradition of Dr. Martin Luther King, Jr. to promote a modern civil rights agenda that includes the fight for one standard of justice, decency and equal opportunities for all people regardless of race, religion, ethnicity, citizenship, criminal record, economic status, gender, gender expression, or sexuality."

I had to step back to take all that in. This group was promoting justice for everyone—not just one group of people. I thought they mainly worked with Black folks, and maybe they do, but just the fact that their mission statement takes care to include all groups of people really impressed me. That is exactly how I feel we should all be doing things—working to give everyone equal opportunity regardless of differences. I get so tired of people being identified by their skin color or their mannerisms or who they love. The whole reason the United States is so great is that it is a melting pot from everywhere, with all types of people. Holding on to prejudices and preconceived notions of people is not only deconstructive but also potentially fatal.

The other areas of focus for NAN include criminal justice reform, police accountability, crisis intake and victim assistance, voting rights, corporate responsibility and pension diversity, youth leadership, and bridging the digital divide. I also looked into the history of the organization, because even though it was doing great work and Reverend Al Sharpton was fronting the group, I wanted to make sure it had a good reputation in the community. I found out that Sharpton created the group after he was stabbed during a protest march.

I know Al Sharpton has his supporters and his denouncers, just like any other public figure, but I think anyone who starts an organization based on such a personal ordeal is at least doing things for the right reasons. The fact that it has grown so large since it began in 1991 demonstrates how important and necessary this group's work has been. I just can't imagine some of the cases they have dealt with and the issues that have plagued so many people.

Armed with that information about the group, I decided that it couldn't hurt to take Cynthia up on her invitation to join her, Al, and the others at their Saturday meeting. They have a rally at least one day a week, sometimes even more if something is happening in the community. So they asked me to come join them at the New York–based organization's NAN office in Harlem, and they even sent a car for me to make sure I could get there.

The first one was the Saturday after Eric died. The funeral hadn't been held yet. I saw Cynthia and talked to Reverend Al, and there were several other members of our family in attendance. As I sat there, I watched as Al preached and several others spoke. In each person, I could see the passion and conviction as they talked about the issue of police brutality in our community. Each person had a story about how they had been harassed and intimidated by the police, very similar to what happened to Eric.

Since the incident on Bay Street had just occurred, everyone was raw with emotion, me most of all. Hearing those stories and realizing just how universal Eric's situation was gave me a sense of relief that it wasn't just my son who went through this, but then I felt guilty because I certainly didn't like that others were experiencing it too. I knew the issue was real in our streets, but I never understood just how everyone seemed to be affected in some way. If they weren't the ones being harassed, they had a relative or friend who was. It just made me so sad that things had gotten this bad, that the police felt that this kind of behavior was necessary and justified. Something about the system was definitely broken because folks should not be treated this way in their own neighborhoods.

People live somewhere they can afford, where they feel comfortable, and in a place that they think is the best situation for their family. Finding out that they are having trouble almost daily as they live in their community just didn't sit right with me. Some of the people spoke of being afraid to walk alone because there were no potential witnesses around and they felt even less safe. But it wasn't the neighborhood they feared—it was the police.

Something had happened along the way. Somehow, with that "broken windows" policy and whatever other "strategies" the city came up with and forced on its officers, they lost the very core of their mission—to serve and protect. It's almost as if people like us were not on an equal playing field, that we weren't treated like everyone else. It felt like Black and Brown folks were the enemy. That didn't feel good, and it didn't feel right. Just as I was amazed by the stories these people shared, I was equally impressed by their actions. They were out in the streets, mobilizing folks to do something. They were marching or picketing or contacting representatives. Whatever it was, they were all getting involved.

That alone was impressive, but it was even more real because they talked of their families and their jobs and they all had full, busy lives, but still they marched. Still they stood in the cold or the rain to make sure they were heard. I think that seemed to be the missing piece of the puzzle. Folks in the community didn't feel important, they didn't feel they were being heard, and they didn't feel like they mattered.

Somewhere along the way, while they were getting married and starting careers and having children, they realized that they were feeling less and less like they were part of their own community. They started to feel like the enemy, like they were doing something wrong just because of what they looked like or where they chose to live. So, despite being so busy, they carved out time to become active and to take a stand. That's easier said than done.

I sat there wondering how they did it. Here I was, working full-time; even with no children living at home, I didn't feel like I had a lot of free time. With family functions, running the house, and my job, I couldn't image grabbing a sign and marching at city hall. As I listened to the speakers, I realized that they didn't have the time, either. They were all busy and stretched thin, but the thing was, they didn't feel like they had a choice. It was their responsibility as residents to do something—anything—to make their neighborhood a better place for their family. That was an a-ha moment for me.

I'd lived through the civil rights movement, and I'd seen our people work hard for change. I guess maybe with raising a family and working, I didn't really think about getting involved. Maybe I had gotten too comfortable, like a lot of people. It's not as if I thought things were perfect by any means, but I didn't think that there was anything someone like me could do to make a difference. Sitting there in that meeting, despite the fact that I still hadn't totally processed my son's death, I started to understand that maybe it's our responsibility to figure out what each of us can do to contribute. But what could a lady like me do?

Every Saturday, NAN continued to send me a ride, and I continued to attend the rallies. Sometimes other family members joined me, and sometimes they didn't. Still, I went. It was like adjusting the focus on a camera. At first things were fuzzy, but the more I went back and the more I listened, the clearer things became. I was learning so much about what people were doing and the responses they were getting. They shared their challenges, their frustrations, and the best part, their successes. I could just see how proud they were when they made progress, even if it was just a small step. The fact that they were able to actually get someone's attention and make something happen was amazing and inspiring. That showed me that it was possible, even for someone like me.

In August, only a month after "that day," Al Sharpton and the people at NAN organized a huge march on Staten Island. It was much bigger than the impromptu one the day after Eric died. There were thousands in attendance, and the atmosphere was so inspiring. Seeing all those people, all kinds of people of every color, come together to demand justice for my son was just amazing. I saw for myself what can happen when people are mobilized.

Eric's murder had been the main topic all over the city for weeks. Everyone was shocked by the viral videos, and it was the topic of conversation no matter where I went. Many tragedies happen in New York City every day, but this was the first time I'd seen one that seemed to take hold of the city and not let go. I guess it was because those videos were impossible to avoid and seeing brutality before their eyes meant that this kind of behavior, this treatment of people, could no longer be ignored. Previously, there might be a mention on the news or talk in the community, but then it would burn off like a heavy morning fog.

This time, with that visual evidence circulating around the world, folks sitting on their comfortable couches or hunched over morning coffee in their work cubicles could watch the video and see for themselves how people were being treated out in the streets. It was no longer a thirty-second news story or a paragraph on the crime blog. It was real life. Every city has an area like Bay Street and a park like Thompsonville, and people like Eric and Ramsey and Taisha. This was not a Staten Island problem, or even a New York problem. It was a problem that affected the entire country.

Everyone could relate to the hopelessness and sheer brutality Eric faced as he fought for his life, as he fought to be *heard*. He was just so frustrated with the constant harassment, the fact that they routinely took his money, and the intimidation tactics they used. He felt like he was trapped, and that he had to take a stand. However, the more he protested, the more they closed in on him. I could just hear the frustration in his voice. That's why I couldn't watch the whole thing. I will not allow that to be the last image I have of my son.

Seeing the commitment of the folks who showed up for the march gave me hope that maybe things would change and this wouldn't happen to anyone else. These people had seen what can happen during a police confrontation, even when you stay peaceful. There were guards from NAN and uniformed and plainclothes police making sure the event stayed peaceful. Emotions were running high, and rightly so. However, we all agreed that there was no room for violence here. We had seen enough violence. Now it was time for change.

I stayed close to Al as we marched down the street alongside family, friends, and others. When we reached the stage, several people made powerful, impactful speeches. Al Sharpton asked those police officers a rhetorical question: "When does your humanity kick in?" There were even retired NYPD officers there who spoke in support of better police training and new strategies to ensure that this kind of incident didn't happen again. If you see me in any of those videos, I'm usually standing with Al, to show support for the cause, and just trying to keep my emotions in check.

You have to remember, I was a happy little homebody before all of this happened, so being suddenly thrust in the middle of this cyclone of activity was very disorienting. I was going along with it, but I wasn't really sure what I was supposed to do or how I was expected to act. What were the rules? What was the protocol? I had no idea. I just did the best I could to try to manage my emotions and take it all in.

I got emotional a lot, especially at the beginning. At first it was because I had to relive Eric's last day on earth, and it was incredibly painful. Going through it once almost destroyed me, so to keep hearing about it and talking about it over and over practically tore me apart. I also got emotional for another reason: Seeing all those people devoting their time to seeking justice for Eric filled me with an almost indescribable joy. These folks, of all races, were sincere in their devotion to helping make things better. Seeing their dedication and hearing their words of strength and determination touched me to the core. I was so relieved that everyone was coming together to demand change, to demand justice, and to demand accountability.

I left that day feeling something I didn't think I would feel for a long time: I felt hopeful. The positive energy flowed from that crowd of people and wrapped around me like a warm blanket. It lifted my spirit and filled my soul in a way that I'd never experienced. How could these strangers have such an impact on me? It was such a welcome surprise that I started to realize the power of mobilization and unity.

In December 2014, we received the devastating news that the New York grand jury had decided not to indict anyone involved in my son's murder. Not one single person was held responsible or accountable. To make matters more frustrating, everything was done behind closed doors, and no documents were shared with us. Everything was supposedly kept confidential to protect those who testified. I'm not sure why that was because everyone I knew who testified said that they were happy to share what they said.

Taisha Allen said that when she testified, she felt rushed and didn't think they were even listening to what she had to say. She also said they kept reinterpreting her words. She felt like it was a waste of her time; they had already decided what they were going to do.

That could be true because all of the law enforcement divisions work together, side by side, every day. The prosecutors are local, so they work with the police officers and the rest of law enforcement. Then they are put in a position to decide whether they are going to charge the officers involved in an incident, and it doesn't make sense. Al Sharpton said that the prosecutors should come from somewhere else, that prosecutors should be brought in to review the evidence and make determinations. It's just so difficult to understand because grand juries almost always take the recommendation of the prosecutors, so why didn't they recommend anything? It's hard to know because everything is classified. The one thing I do know is that my son is dead and no one is being held accountable. As a parent and a mother, I just find that reprehensible. How can I, in good conscience, not do something in my son's name? How can I just let them get away with his murder?

After the disappointing ruling, we all gathered at the NAN office in Harlem. Al was there, and Cynthia Davis, my family, and lots of other concerned citizens. Al declared it "a national crisis." He asked, "How many have to die before people understand this is a reality that

America has to come to terms with? No secret grand jury with local prosecutors will stop people from demanding answers. We are not advocating violence—we are asking that police violence stop."

I braced myself for the public reaction, and, as expected, it was swift and loud. It wasn't just New York City that was stunned by the ruling but the entire country. Along with the strong reaction locally, there were "Garner protests" in every major city. Unfortunately, there were a few violent incidents, but for the most part it was a united, countrywide, peaceful protest against a horrible decision. Some universities staged "die-ins," where students placed themselves strategically on the lush green lawns in front of academic buildings to illustrate the seriousness and the magnitude of the issue. Major highways were shut down by peaceful marches down streets, over bridges, and up to the steps of city hall. This was in December, but protesters braved the cold, the rain, and the wind. They were not about to let the weather deter them from their mission for justice.

Then it went much further than that. Of course, it took over the social media platforms, but another group showed their support for the cause. Major athletes made their own statements to show solidarity within the rules of their sport and their team. Without showing disrespect or disruption to their sport, they instead decided to get creative.

One of the first NBA players to show disdain for the decision was 2011 MVP Chicago Bulls player Derrick Rose, who wore the words "I can't breathe" on a T-shirt during pregame warmups against the Warriors on December 6. Others joined in soon after, including LeBron James and Kyrie Irving of the Cleveland Cavaliers, who wore similar T-shirts during their pregame warmups against the Nets. Several Nets players wore the message as well, including Jarrett Jack, Alan Anderson, Deron Williams, and Kevin Garnett.

Detroit Lions running back Reggie Bush wore an "I can't breathe" shirt before one of his games. Other NFL players to wear T-shirts with the phrase included Cleveland Browns cornerback Johnson Bademosi, San Diego Chargers linebacker Melvin Ingram, and St. Louis Rams offensive lineman Davin Joseph, who strategically wrote the message on his cleats.

I was worried there might be some backlash in the sports community because previously, to support the protest of yet another grand jury decision not to indict, this time in the Michael Brown case in Ferguson, Missouri, several members of the Rams had entered the field with their hands in the air in the universal "don't shoot" pose. That caused some boos and fan rage in the parking lots following the games. Fortunately, I didn't see any of that with Eric's case.

The sight of those sports figures showing their support meant a lot for several reasons. First, since they are role models for many young children, they set the tone with their behavior, which is why leagues and teams often have strict conduct rules. Seeing them showing their support and dedication to the cause in their own way meant a lot. Plus, it sent a signal to those viewers that just because you are watching entertainment doesn't mean everything else is ignored. Things are still happening in the world, and people are allowed to express their opinions.

Second, the majority of the players showing support were minorities, so they know what it can be like out in those streets and communities. They know the difficulties of growing up Black in America. It's not easy, no matter where you live. It's filled with challenges and struggles regardless of social status or pedigree. Racism in our country is real, and it's pervasive.

You don't escape it because you are in an elevated social class or in a privileged community. It still happens, and it's still hurtful, and most of all, it can still be deadly. That's the message we were working hard to convey, that everyone should be treated equally regardless of their differences. And while NAN fights to protect everyone, at that point the country was dealing with an alarming number of cases where Black and Brown people were being harassed and even killed at the hands of law enforcement. Those challenges exist, even though they shouldn't.

Particularly if you are a minority, you need to be aware and you need to be prepared. Driving while Black, walking while Black, shopping while Black, going to a park while Black, and certainly being out on the sidewalk on Bay Street in the middle of the day while Black can get you killed. There's no denying that, and there's no mistaking the gravity of the situation.

I appreciated the dedication and commitment that sprung up across the country, and I thought that those sports figures, with the highly visible platform and large social reach, were especially helpful and impactful when they took a stand. That also hit home for me because I remember learning about some very pivotal sports moments when I was in high school.

We learned that civil rights and sports have intersected at some very historic times. In the 1936 Olympics, Jesse Owens set the world on fire with his amazing performance in track and field. It was especially impactful because it occurred in Germany during Hitler's rise to power, and it effectively and dramatically blew a hole in the Aryan race theory of superiority. Jesse's epic performance showed the world that there is no better race—just amazing people who succeed because of their skill, determination, and perseverance.

That fact that this Black man made such an indelible mark on the games and was the first American track and field athlete to win four gold medals in a single Olympics was important. It was especially impactful because it happened in Nazi Germany, on their own turf. In addition, it helped elevate public conversation about race and civil rights and the fact that it's about the individual, not a person's race.

I also remembered another Olympic event that I lived through. It was also very impactful. It was the 1968 games held in Mexico City, and at the medal ceremony, after they won gold and bronze medals, two Black athletes named Tommie Smith and John Carlos stood on their raised podiums. As "The Star-Spangled Banner" began to play, they faced the American flag and raised their fists in the "Black Power" symbol to show their solidarity with those around the world who were fighting for human rights. It was very moving for me because that was when the civil rights activities were really gaining momentum in the United States and there was lots of controversy. The two medalists were booed when they left the field and were then removed from the rest of the Olympics that year.

It seems like athletics and political statements have gone on throughout history, so my only hope was that it would somehow raise human consciousness about the issues of police brutality and the injustice that almost always follows those events. If a sports figure can get people to think and to talk, maybe there is hope that change will occur. The only way something like that is going to happen is if people demand it. I had been learning that through those Saturday rallies and marches in the streets.

That quiet voice inside of me started to grow louder and louder. I began to think, *Maybe I can have my voice heard, and maybe people will actually listen.* Maybe this was a way to keep Eric's name out there in the public and keep the incident fresh in people's minds so that they didn't forget. With that line of thinking, I started going to more marches and more rallies and more protests. With Cynthia's encouragement, I stood out in the cold and the rain and the snow. Sometimes it was just her and me, just the two of us, standing in front of the post office on Staten Island, one of the only official buildings we could find. That was all right. I was learning.

You know why I really started to get involved? It might sound odd, but each time I did it, I felt closer to Eric. I felt like I was honoring him, and he was there with me. With each step I took and each sign I made, I could feel him more and more. It was a comfort and a sign of encouragement for me. I know that if he had been here and saw me doing that, he would have been so surprised: "Ma, what are you doing? That's not like you." But then he would have been so proud that I was getting outside of my comfort zone.

I started doing it for him, for his memory, and for his spirit, because it fed my soul and gave me reason to get up in the morning. After a full day of marching and sharing stories about Eric until my voice was raw, I would lie down in bed satisfied that I had done my best that day. Then, before I went to sleep, I would promise Eric that I was going to do that same thing tomorrow, the next day, and the next.

I knew it was too late for Eric, but I realized that I had to try to do everything I could to save other people, especially the children. I had to change my mourning into movement, my pain into purpose, and my sorrow into strategy. At first the publicity and the media and the attention was just too much for me. I wasn't sure I could handle it. Having such a bright spotlight on my personal life was uncomfortable.

Then I realized that I needed to take that discomfort and shift it so that it would motivate me. The more attention I got, the more interview requests I received, and the more reporters that showed up, the more strength I got. I decided that I needed to harness that attention and use that energy for positivity.

At first I wondered who would listen to quiet, reserved Gwen Carr, a great-grandmother from Brooklyn. But even after the grand jury's horrible decision, I was still getting requests to come somewhere to speak or sit on a panel or even tape a television show. To me, that meant this wasn't going away. Unfortunately, there had been several other horrible police incidents, and still Eric's case was on the minds of the public. People refused to give up on him and his memory. The sheer injustice and inhumanity made an impression that was hard to shake.

Realizing that this wasn't going away, I did what I'd promised myself when I was starting to spiral into that hole of depression—find something new to focus on. Here it was, right in front of me. This was my new mission and my purpose. It fulfilled me and gave me the satisfaction that I was truly putting my energy where it had the most impact. I wasn't sitting at home. I was out in the community, on the evening news, and on the radio telling everyone my story.

I would keep Eric's name out there and continue to talk about him. I would make sure his life meant something and show that he was much more than just a Black man in a viral video. He was a caring, compassionate man who had love as wide as the ocean. And it made me feel good to share stories about him because in each interview I was invariably asked, "What was your son like?"

That question always got to me, caused me to stop for a minute and take a breath. I was doing this for Eric, and when I heard someone else say his name, it would just hit me that he was no longer with me. Until then, when I was talking about him, it was like it used to be when he was alive, me bragging on my son. However, when someone asked what he *was* like—well, that would bring reality crashing back down around me.

It's not that I was fooling myself or anything—it was just that I felt so good talking about him and his spirit that I could push reality back for just a minute and escape into a world where my son was still with me. Then I started to realize that he *was* with me, that I could feel his presence. It was more spiritual and soulful than anything else. I just felt full and complete when I spoke about him. His spirit filled me, and as I continued speaking about him, my spirit stayed full and it felt good.

To me, that was the only sign I needed that I was on the right path and doing what I needed to be doing. I still wasn't great at it, at least I didn't think so, but people kept telling me that I was doing a good job. In the beginning, I wanted to be perfect. I wanted to say the right things, wear the right clothes, come across in the right way. I didn't want to be seen as pushy or preachy.

Once, I had to speak in front of a large group, and it was my first big speaking opportunity. I prayed that I would have the strength to do a good job and come across in just the right way. I thought about other speakers I had seen and wished I were more polished like them or used bigger words or had better stories to share. As I continued to pray about it, I think Eric came to me because I heard and felt the spirit.

There was no need to worry about being perfect because there's no such thing. I just needed to trust in myself and be as authentic as I could be. That's how people relate to me and it's the only way I need to be, which is good because it's the only way I know how to be. All of this came out of a horrible situation. I didn't seek it out. I had no interest in getting involved in change before all of this happened. I was happy to just stay at home, go to work, and visit family on the weekends.

At first, after everything happened, I was still employed at the MTA, but as things progressed I realized that I couldn't go back to work. I just couldn't imagine after all that had happened that I would be underground driving a train through the underbelly of the city. I did try, though. One day I felt like I had gotten better, and I went in to work to see how it felt. Everyone was very nice and supportive, but at the end of that day, one of the dispatchers came running out of the office when my train came in. I thought she was going to offer her condolences, but instead she said, "I see your train didn't come in on time, so I marked you ten minutes late." I signed out and went home. I never went back.

I had vacation and other paid time off, and they were very good to me during my time away from work. They even sent papers to me to sign when I couldn't come in and always checked to see how I was doing. So I appreciated them on that level, but I realized that with all I'd been through, it was time for a new chapter in my life.

Things were so much bigger now, and they had taken on a different meaning. Getting called out for being ten minutes late on a train run was just something that I couldn't deal with. Eric's death overshadowed everything else, and everything else seemed so much smaller in comparison. It just didn't have the same importance. I guess my perspective had changed . . . a lot.

It was time for me to use whatever means I could to spread the message about my son and the horrible event that ended his life. I didn't know if I could make a real difference, but I did know that I could try. After attending the NAN events and watching Reverend Al, I had learned from the best, so I could do it my own way. With their support and the support of my family and friends, I stepped out of my comfort zone and into the public eye.

To be honest, it felt good doing it based on my own decision and not because I was forced to due to the circumstances. It was important to me that I did it when I was ready and when I felt comfortable. Most important, I waited until I felt like I had a sign from my son that this was the path I should take. It was still scary, and I wasn't exactly sure what I was getting into.

At this stage of my life, it's probably unusual to start a new chapter like this, but it feels right, and it feels important. I'm not taking up a new hobby; I'm trying to bring about real change that will help others live better lives. I'm also hoping that through it all, during this journey, I'll be able to see some justice for Eric's death. As a mother, I owe it to him and to his brother Emery to do whatever I can. I know I can't bring them back, but by talking about them I can keep them with me. That makes me feel like I'm doing what is right for me and for them.

When I checked back at the National Action Network website to remind myself of their mission, I saw that they added my son's name to their crisis intake and victim assistance section: "NAN has led the fight against police misconduct and other injustices by ensuring that those whose rights are violated are brought to justice. NAN's efforts were on display in response to events involving the police sodomy of Abner Louima; the police killings of Amadou Diallo, Sean Bell, Ramarley Graham, and *Eric Garner* among others; and the killing of Trayvon Martin by a neighborhood 'watchman.' We also offer legal assistance through Legal Night and referrals to clients through our Crisis Intake and National Crisis Center, headquartered at our House of Justice in Harlem."

Gwen Carr with daughter Ellisha and grandchildren.
(Unless otherwise stated, photos are from the author's
personal collection.)

Garner and Flagg families together at Eric's repast.

Eric participating in Coney Island House's third annual Remembrance Day.

Eric on Easter Sunday going to church with family in 1987.

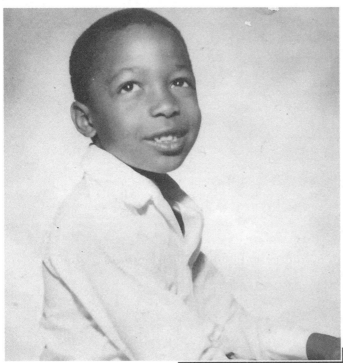

Eric at five years old.

Eric's sixth-grade
graduation picture.

Eric with younger brother Emery.

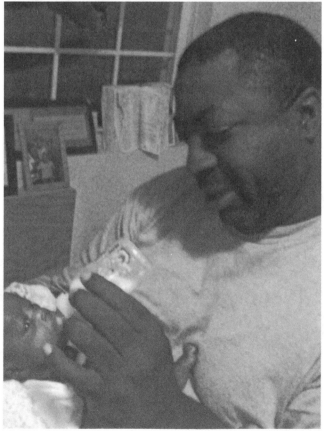

The last time Eric held his little baby girl, Legacy, who was three months old when he passed.

Eric in junior high school.

GOOD Luck from JOSE

Eric, Good Luck in High School. I know you will succeed. Remember to get that piece of paper (diploma) you've been waiting for. Remember the J.H.S. could you resisted! You can do it! I'll help you in H.S. at Graduation it Mr. Terrill

MRS. WARNER
MR. RUSSEL
MRS. BOOTH
MRS. JOSEPH
MS. SOLOMON

Eric's junior high school yearbook.

Eric and Ellisha with godsister Tasha having fun. Ellisha is on the left.

Eric's high school picture senior year.

Gwen and Ellisha visiting the DOJ in 2017.

Ellisha, Gwen, and Eric in Gowanus housing in downtown Brooklyn.

Gwen and her granddaughter Chayla being escorted to Eric's funeral.

Gwen at a roundtable discussion on NYPD discipline.

President Barack Obama and Gwen in Washington, DC, at a town hall meeting in July 2016.

Al Sharpton and Gwen at the second annual commemorative march of Eric's death.

Gwen gives a speech at Prospect Park in Brooklyn.

A friend edited a photo so that Gwen could be by her son's side once again.

Gwen speaks at a rally in front of the governor's office in Albany, New York, in support of an executive order for a special prosecutor in local police misconduct cases.

Hillary Clinton, Gwen Carr, Maxine Waters, and other supporters in Los Angeles during the presidential campaign.

Gwen Carr and Nadia Fischer meet author/director Antwone Fisher.

Gwen visits Eric's grave. (Courtesy of Darnell Felder.)

# Chapter 6

─────────────○─────────────

# The Mothers of the Movement

You may encounter many defeats, but you must not be defeated. In fact, it may be necessary to encounter the defeats, so you can know who you are, what you can rise from, how you can still come out of it.

—Maya Angelou

I ATTENDED AN EVENT IN THE fall of 2014 that changed my life. It was the Congressional Black Caucus (CBC) convention on September 19, in Washington, DC, along with friends I'd made from the National Action Network. While there, I met someone else who became an important person in my life. A little more than two years before Eric died, seventeen-year-old Trayvon Martin was shot in Sanford, Florida, by a neighborhood watch volunteer. I had heard a lot about that case, and it had made such an impression on me because the boy was a teenager and because it seemed so senseless, like Eric's death.

At the CBC convention I met Sybrina Fulton, Trayvon's mother. She seemed so poised. She was so very nice and giving when we spoke and shared our stories. We'd only seen each other in the news, so it was a little strange meeting in real life, but that went away quickly. She shared how things had been going for her and how she had been handling the attention, which was very helpful

to me. Plus, she has been involved in activism herself and gave me
some advice: "Miss Gwen, a lot of people will ask you to do a lot
of things, and sometimes you just have to say no." That was good
advice, because I was still learning the ins and outs of this activism
stuff and what it was like being in the public eye.

I also met Lezley McSpadden, the mother of Michael Brown,
who just a month before the convention had been killed by Ferguson, Missouri, police at a convenience store. It was refreshing to
talk to the two mothers because they were in a situation very similar
to mine. The three of us were all members of an unfortunate club,
a club that no one would ever choose to join. Our sons had died at
the hands of "law enforcement" in one way or another, and while
the circumstances were different, the resulting pain was the same.
At first it felt strange that we were connected by our grief, but as
we got to know each other, we realized that we had other things in
common as well. I also found that being able to talk and share with
these ladies made me feel a little better, that maybe I wasn't out
here all alone. These women were also getting involved, which was
the reason they decided to attend the convention. We all hoped to
glean some advice and tools and strategies that we could use when
we went back home to our community activism.

That felt a little odd too, calling myself an activist. Whenever
I heard that word it conjured up images of the 1960s and Dr. King
and protests and handmade signs. I'm sure it was my own stereo-
typing, but I just felt like an activist was so informed and driven and
determined. I didn't feel like I was in that league. Maybe I would get
there. I wasn't sure. I didn't know if that was even what I wanted.
It had only been a couple of months since my son's passing, and
everything was all so new. I didn't feel like an activist. I just felt
like myself trying to get out there and make people think. Maybe it
would get better with time.

I guess if you have a lot of money, you can pay people to help
train you on what to do and say and how to act, but I'm not that
way, so I just do it the best I can. It was definitely inspiring to see all
the people brought together by that convention. Their focus was on
ensuring justice for all, decreasing gaps in education, and promoting

economic security for all people. Each year it is a four-day event at the Walter E. Washington Convention Center in DC. There were thousands there, and I noticed that a lot of the programs focused on young Black people and their future, which I found encouraging.

It was somewhat overwhelming that first time because there were receptions, breakfasts, exhibits, gospel events, jazz concerts, prayer breakfasts—all leading up to the Phoenix Awards Dinner that closed out the convention. Just like the presidential inaugurations in that city, there are also lots of receptions and networking events in bars, restaurants, and meeting halls all around town. There was a lot to take in and a lot to learn, but that was OK. I was ready for it. Things were starting to click as I saw the power of organization and mobilization.

To continue educating myself, I found out a little about the CBC that puts on this annual event:

> Since its establishment in 1971, the Congressional Black Caucus (CBC) has been committed to using the full Constitutional power, statutory authority, and financial resources of the federal government to ensure that African Americans and other marginalized communities in the United States have the opportunity to achieve the American Dream. As part of this commitment, the CBC has fought for the past 46 years to empower these citizens and address their legislative concerns by pursuing a policy agenda that includes but is not limited to the following:
>
> - reforming the criminal justice system and eliminating barriers to reentry;
> - combatting voter suppression;
> - expanding access to world-class education from pre-k through postsecondary level;
> - expanding access to quality, affordable health care and eliminating racial health disparities;
> - expanding access to 21st century technologies, including broadband;
> - strengthening protections for workers and expanding access to full, fairly-compensated employment;

- expanding access to capital, contracts, and counseling for minority-owned businesses; and
- promoting U.S. foreign policy initiatives in Africa and other countries that are consistent with the fundamental right of human dignity.

For the 115th Congress, the CBC has a historic forty-nine members in the U.S. House of Representatives and the U.S. Senate, representing seventy-eight million Americans, 24 percent of the total U.S. population, and seventeen million African Americans—41 percent of the U.S. African American population. In addition, the CBC represents almost a fourth of the House Democratic Caucus.

The CBC is engaged at the highest levels of Congress with members who serve in House leadership and are full committee and subcommittee ranking members. Representative James E. Clyburn (D-SC) serves as the assistant Democratic leader in the House, six CBC members serve as ranking members on full House committees, and thirty-one CBC members serve as ranking members on House and Senate subcommittees.

While the CBC has predominately been made up of members of the Democratic Party, the founding members of the Caucus envisioned a nonpartisan organization. Consequently, the CBC has a long history of bipartisan collaboration and members who are both Democrat and Republican.

As founding member Representative William L. Clay Sr. said when the CBC was established, "Black people have no permanent friends, no permanent enemies . . . just permanent interests."

The next year, 2015, I was officially retired from the MTA, where I had worked for twenty-two years as a conductor and then a train operator. It took some getting used to since going to work had been part of my routine for so long. I felt a little lost at first. I was already without my son, and now I no longer had a job. In my mind, I kept thinking that once I got back to work, things would settle down and get back to normal.

I wasn't sure what normal meant anymore, but I knew I just wanted to get back to a routine, a daily schedule where I knew what I was going to do and when. That type of structure can be very helpful when dealing with tragic situations. It helps to provide something else to focus on and somewhere to channel that pent-up energy. So when I retired, it meant that my time was now truly my own. It was up to me to decide how I would spend it.

I certainly didn't plan to fade into the background, especially after that energizing convention I'd attended a few months back. Since that time, I'd kept in touch with Sybrina and Lezley, and I was enjoying that friendship. I didn't know the women very well, but I felt an instant connection because of our shared experiences. I kept thinking about all the powerful people I had seen and met— the members of Congress, community leaders, and so many others. They were working for change and that energized me, which I guess is the ultimate goal of those conventions. And it worked on me.

I also began meeting other women who had gone through similar ordeals as me, Sybrina, and Lezley. There was Maria Hamilton, whose son, Dontre, was shot and killed by police in Milwaukee in April 2014. There was Lucy McBath: her son, Jordan Davis, was only seventeen when a man shot him outside of a convenience store in Jacksonville, Florida, over a dispute about playing a car stereo too loudly in 2012. Cleopatra Cowley-Pendleton's daughter, Hadiya, was fifteen years old when she was shot at Harsh Park in Kenwood, Chicago, a week after performing at Obama's second inauguration in 2013.

Like most of America, I had heard about these incidents, some more than others. I'm not sure how that happens, but some seemed to garner more attention from the press than others. Some linger while others seem to fade from the public more quickly. I suppose it depends on what else is happening in the country. However, I did realize that as more people began recording these incidents, they really started to get more coverage from the press.

Hearing some of those horrible stories was of course upsetting and disturbing, and when they were accompanied by the undeniable images, it just amplified everything. People kept saying that it was for the better because that meant more attention and focus, which could ultimately result in changes that would help stop the deaths. That was probably true, but it was difficult to see and hear more and more cases.

Meeting these women and hearing their stories usually left me speechless. I was trying to get over that habit that I had, to retreat and stay quiet, but it was not easy. I understood the pain these brave ladies felt, and it hurt me to see them still dealing with it years later. I think that's because I saw my future in them. I had been telling myself that things were going to get better and time would help to ease the pain; the horrible images would gradually fade into some area of my brain where it wasn't the only thing I could think about. Then, after meeting the other women, I realized that was just wishful thinking. It was obvious that this was my future. I would always have this pain to deal with, just like these strong women were doing. It would never get easier.

That's when it really started to click for me. Why did it have to get easier? That would just lull me into complacency, into acceptance about what happened to Eric. I did not want that to happen. I shared a commonality with these women, and I could see that they had already come to the realization that they had to do something. Sitting on the sidelines was not an option. Hoping things would get better was not an option. More deaths were not an option.

In April 2015, Representative Hakeem Jeffries, a Democrat representing New York, held a press conference to announce that he was introducing federal legislation to ban police chokeholds. It had been less than a year since Eric's death, so I was very excited that some type of change was possible. The bill was called the Excessive Use of Force Prevention Act, and I was asked to join him outside of One Police Plaza in Manhattan as he made the announcement to the press. Cynthia Davis came along with me as she continued to mentor me and help me through this new chapter of my life. Minister Kirsten John Foy from the National Action Network was there as well.

The goal of the bill was to specifically define what a chokehold is, because, as I had learned, if everything is not very clearly spelled out, it's open to interpretation. This legislation defined the chokehold as "the application of any pressure to the throat or windpipe which may prevent or hinder breathing or reduce the intake of air." Representative Jeffries had done a lot of research and said that there were police departments in many cities that prohibited the use of chokeholds, but there was no law against it at the federal level.

He pointed out that the majority of police departments don't have a specific policy on chokeholds, and some only go as far as to "discourage" their use. I just hoped after everyone saw Eric on video receiving a chokehold that it registered with people just how deadly it is. Representative Jeffries pointed out what had become glaringly obvious—the police department policies were obviously not effective at eliminating the chokehold's use by officers.

There was another important reason for the legislation. Since the New York grand jury had refused to bring about any charges, our only other hope was the U.S. Department of Justice. They were currently reviewing Eric's case to determine whether his civil rights were violated by the NYPD. I was told that it was a long shot, but at that point I didn't care. I would take that over nothing. The state of New York had let us down, so I hoped that maybe something would happen at the federal level, and I knew that this bill could help the Department of Justice by giving it clear authority to intervene in cases where the chokehold was used.

As I said at the press conference, why should someone be choked to death? Especially when they are unarmed? I felt that this was a step in the right direction, and I was honored to be a part of it. That was also one of the first press conferences that I attended by myself. Before that, I usually had several family members with me to provide strength and support, which I desperately needed. This time, I was a little nervous at first, especially when I was asked to give my opinion, but after I spoke I felt much better. I didn't prepare anything ahead of time. I just said what was in my heart.

Everyone assured me that I had done well, and I appreciated that because this mission began to feel much more natural to me than it had at first. With each event and each speaking opportunity, I became more at ease and more confident. I wasn't totally there yet, because I still felt out of place among these people who had so much more experience than I did. However, standing up at that microphone and hearing my words amplified and watching reporters record what I had to say helped me realize that I did have something to add to the conversation. They were interested in my words and my experiences.

Another civil rights tragedy befell a major city that same month. In April 2015, a twenty-five-year-old Black man named Freddie Gray was fatally injured while being transported in a police van. His death sparked citywide riots in his hometown of Baltimore. It had still not even been a year since my son had died, and I think people were just so tired of the treatment we were receiving at the hands of police. I was sad for the riots because I didn't think violence was the answer, but I did understand their frustrations.

In the short amount of time I had spent working to create change, I realized how slowly things moved along. I wanted things to happen right away, but once I got educated on how things work, I saw that to get something done and to get the cooperation of others, especially those in power, you had to follow established procedures and work within their guidelines. Otherwise you were just spinning your wheels.

During April, the National Action Network held its seventeenth annual national convention at the Sheraton New York Hotel. It was just after the fiftieth anniversary of the civil rights marches in Selma, Alabama. This meeting was more political because the presidential election was coming up in 2016 and candidates were starting to be more visible as they jockeyed for position in their respective parties. Candidates such as Ben Carson, Martin O'Malley, and Bernie Sanders were there as well as New York mayor Bill de Blasio and many other politicians. There were also many celebrities involved, such as director Lee Daniels and actor Anthony Anderson.

I was on a panel along with some of the other mothers and family members of police victims, including Sybrina Fulton (Trayvon Martin), Lezley McSpadden (Michael Brown), Valerie Bell (Sean Bell), and Samaria Rice, mother of Tamir, a twelve-year-old shot by police officers. We were often referred to as "grassroots activists," and I was becoming more comfortable with the term. I guess I was officially an activist.

At each of these events, and with the guidance of the people at NAN, and especially Cynthia Davis, I would meet yet another mother whose child had been killed. There were just so many of us, and we all had that one connection—we had all lost a child to violence, often at the hands of the police. It never got easier to meet someone else and hear their story. It was much different talking to them directly as opposed to what was reported on the news. Hearing from them how their lives had been impacted was nothing short of heartbreaking.

But each time I heard another story, I realized that's where our power was. That was the strength all of us mothers shared. We were able to humanize our children and show that they were much more than a news headline. Our children were people with hopes and dreams just like anyone else, and we all agreed that they deserved to be remembered for more than just their violent ending. That was our mission as parents, to not only help to bring about change but also tell the story of our children and give them the respect they deserved.

While there were sometimes other family members in attendance who were related to those who had died, it was the mothers who really got people's attention. I think it was for a couple of reasons. First, it is often a reality that many Black families are led by mothers since there is not always a father in the home. So, just by sheer numbers, there are usually more mothers at the events. Second, a mother's love is universal. Everyone can understand and relate to the powerful connection that is shared by a mother and her child.

At these events, when there were several of us mothers present, we began to be referred to as "the mothers" and then "the Mothers of the Movement." We weren't an actual organized group, but we happened to be at many of the same functions, working for the same thing: justice.

I joined a large group that went to the New York State Capitol in Albany to demand that the governor sign an order that would bring

in special prosecutors to handle police shootings of individuals. I
was in the company of yet another mother I'd met—Valerie Bell,
whose son Sean was shot and killed by police in 2006, on his wed-
ding day, in Queens, New York. There were others in attendance as
well, and we all had the same mission: to demand that Governor
Cuomo meet with us to discuss our issues. We had tried to meet
with him in the past, but he would not make himself available. He
avoided us. This time, with a large group of us outside, we were not
going to be ignored any longer.

Maybe the frustrations I saw in Baltimore helped to fuel my
determination, but I was not going to leave there without speaking
to the governor. After what I had been through and what so many
others like Valerie had experienced, we deserved to at least meet
with our own governor. Just because he might not like what we had
to say didn't mean he should avoid us. His job is to listen to all citizens, not just ones he agrees with.

We were all pleasantly surprised when, after first denying us,
we were informed that the governor would make time to meet with
us that afternoon to hear what we had to say. As promised, we were
escorted into a room where we met with the governor and some
of his staff members. He listened to our concerns, and I was very
clear with my message: I did not feel like my son had received a fair
ruling from the grand jury, and it was time for changes to be made
regarding police incidents.

I was glad that he listened, and I thought that it was a move in
the right direction. He even promised that he would be willing to
meet again to discuss the matter in more detail. That was logical
since we had basically shown up unannounced. I looked forward to
a more organized meeting to discuss the topic further. Beyond that,
the meeting gave me renewed hope that things weren't as impossible as I had initially thought. Speaking out could actually make
a difference. It was obvious that things were going to take some
time, but I felt like we were laying the groundwork for something to
happen, and I was right in the middle of it all.

Those were serious times, and most of the events, despite everyone being cordial and welcoming, had a somber tone. People

were reverent in their dealings with me and the other mothers in attendance. They were considerate and polite and serious. Dealing with death, as I was still learning, was an ongoing process for me and others. This was my third time experiencing someone so close to me dying, and it didn't get any easier along the way. So I was mostly invited to events like that. There were roundtable discussions, community involvement events, rallies, luncheons, conventions, and so on. They just kept coming, and I kept attending.

There were opportunities for other events along the way as well. I think folks wanted to show some appreciation for what the other mothers and I were doing, and they knew that any event we attended would help bring more exposure to the cause, even if it was a concert. On May 10, I was invited to Baltimore to see Prince perform. It was somewhat related to my mission because he was holding it for the fans in Baltimore after what they had been through with the riots. It was called Prince's Rally 4 Peace, and it was to benefit the community. He was intent on bringing some entertainment to the city as well as raising money for local charities.

The concert was pulled together on short notice, but you would have never known by the sheer magnitude of it. There were so many people there, and it was amazing to see everyone coming together and celebrating after what had happened there. Prince even wrote a song about the city and ending police brutality. At the concert, I was able to meet so many fascinating people, including Alicia Keys, JAY-Z and his mother, and Beyoncé. They were all very gracious, and I truly enjoyed meeting them.

That July was the first anniversary of Eric's death, and it made me reflect on the year I'd had. Looking back, I couldn't believe all that had happened. I was still trying to get used to the fact that Eric was not around, that he wasn't calling to check on me or coming over to the house just to talk and catch me up on his life. We had such a close relationship when it was taken away so abruptly and violently; it didn't seem real. Even after a year of not seeing him, it didn't seem like that was my reality.

However, after taking stock of what I'd been through, I had surprised not only others but also myself with all the events I attended and the speeches I'd made. A quiet woman like me was speaking out, and people were listening. I was still getting used to that. It's one thing when someone sets out to make changes and get active in their community. It's much different when it is basically thrust upon you. All of this was dropped in my lap, and it was up to me how I wanted to handle it. I could have just hidden my head in the sand, stayed inside my modest home, and dealt with things myself.

I didn't do that. When I realized that might be my reality, I took action to make sure that I did something unexpected. I got involved. It was very slow at first and took a lot of coaxing and encouragement from my family and experts like Cynthia, but with that help and confidence, I was able to keep Eric's name alive and ensure that it meant something. He was so much more than a Black man in a T-shirt on Bay Street. He was a beautiful person, and he was my son.

The fact that I was able to move forward the way I did was something that I allowed myself to be proud of. It's not that I was innocent a year ago, but I did not understand anything about government and politics and legislation or any of that. I never imagined that I would be meeting with the governor and championing legislation that could potentially benefit people across the country. It was somewhat mind boggling to think about it like that.

That was the very reason why I decided at the beginning to just take things one step at a time. I didn't think too far down the road about what would happen if this bill passed or if we didn't get to meet with that politician. I couldn't spend my energy like that. Plus, if I did think too much about it, it was overwhelming, and I'd start to think that I couldn't do it. When I'd be asked to speak in front of people, I didn't focus on it too much because if I did, I'd internalize it and work myself up. If the speech was a few months away, I'd mark it on the calendar and then not think about it.

I decided to just handle things as they came along and deal with them as best I could. I focused on the tasks in front of me, and things worked out better that way. For me, slow and steady was the best strategy, and it seemed to be working. I thought after a year of talking about Eric the interest would die down and people would start moving on to something else, but that's not what happened.

A large part of that could be attributed to those mothers who were out there before I was. They weren't doing many things together, but individually they were having their own rallies and marches and working in their communities to bring about much-needed change. They gave me strength, and when we all came together we fed off each other's energy. We weren't necessarily best friends, but we were all connected in our passion, and that was enough.

In July 2015, almost exactly a year to the day of Eric's death, Governor Cuomo signed an executive order that said he was appointing an attorney general as a special prosecutor for cases where people died at the hands of the police. I attended the announcement along with several other mothers, including Iris Baez, Margarita Rosario, Constance Malcolm, and Hawa Bah. We released a joint statement that read:

> For decades, our families and those of other New Yorkers killed by police have faced repeated injustices, not only losing family members to police violence by those tasked with serving and protecting but also being failed by local district attorneys not holding officers accountable to the law for those deaths. Many of us have been calling for a special prosecutor for decades, so this reform stems from the legacies of New Yorkers whose unjust deaths go back a long time and the leadership of our families. Today, Governor Cuomo is listening to our voices and those of other New Yorkers who support equal justice to enact an important reform to end this conflict of interest. Nothing will bring back the lives of our loved ones, and this was never simply about our families—it was about all those who come after us because we so deeply understand the pain and heartache of losing a loved one and then having their life not matter within our justice system. While New York takes national leadership with this reform, there remains much work to be done to ensure our children and family members are no longer unjustly killed by police in the first place. We hope to work with Governor Cuomo and other leaders in moving New York forward to build upon today's important step to end the discriminatory and abusive policing that threatens our families and communities.

I can tell you that was an amazing feeling. I'm not saying that I was the one responsible for it, but I did work hard to make something happen, so it was exciting and rewarding to see that something was finally going to be done. Of course, I knew it wasn't a perfect solution and it wouldn't solve all the problems, but it was a start, and it was more than we had the day before.

Lots of folks had been involved, and many spoke out in support of the action. People from the National Action Network and the NAACP spoke out about it, including Attorney General Eric Schneiderman, Congressman Hakeem Jeffries, several senators, and even Russell Simmons.

Specifically, the executive order says:

## EXECUTIVE ORDER

### A SPECIAL PROSECUTOR TO INVESTIGATE AND PROSECUTE MATTERS RELATING TO THE DEATHS OF CIVILIANS CAUSED BY LAW ENFORCEMENT OFFICERS.

**WHEREAS,** the Constitution of the State of New York obliges the Governor to take care that the laws of New York are faithfully executed; and

**WHEREAS,** I have solemnly sworn, pursuant to Article 13, Section 1 of the Constitution, to support the Constitution and faithfully discharge the duties of the office of Governor; and

**WHEREAS,** there have been recent incidents involving the deaths of unarmed civilians that have challenged the public's confidence and trust in our system of criminal justice; and

**WHEREAS,** public concerns have been raised that such incidents cannot be prosecuted at the local level without conflict or bias, or the public perception of conflict or bias; and

**WHEREAS,** it is necessary to ensure that a full, reasoned, and independent investigation and prosecution of any such incident is conducted without conflict or bias, or the perception of conflict or bias; and

**WHEREAS,** the foregoing compels me to conclude that my constitutional obligations provide that in cases where an issue of a real or perceived conflict of interest exists, and to ensure full confidence in our system of criminal justice, a special prosecutor should be appointed with respect to such incidents. Such appointment of a special prosecutor will supersede in all ways the authority and jurisdiction of a county district attorney to manage, interpret, prosecute or inquire about such incidents; and

**NOW, THEREFORE, I, ANDREW M. CUOMO,** Governor of the State of New York, by virtue of the authority vested in me by the Constitution and Laws of the State of New York, and particularly by subdivision 2 of section 63 of the Executive Law, hereby require the Attorney General (hereinafter, the "special prosecutor") to investigate, and if warranted, prosecute certain matters involving the death of an unarmed civilian, whether in custody or not, caused by a law enforcement officer, as listed in subdivision 34 of section 1.20 of the Criminal Procedure Law. The special prosecutor may also investigate and prosecute in such instances where, in his opinion, there is a significant question as to whether the civilian was armed and dangerous at the time of his or her death;

**FURTHER,** for any matter covered herein, the special prosecutor shall have the powers and duties specified in subdivisions 2 and 8 of section 63 of the Executive Law for purposes of this Order, and shall possess and exercise all the prosecutorial powers necessary to investigate, and if warranted, prosecute the incident. The special prosecutor's jurisdiction will displace and supersede the jurisdiction of the county district attorney where the incident occurred; and such county district attorney shall have only the powers and duties designated to him or her by the special prosecutor as specified in subdivision 2 of section 63 of the Executive Law;

**FURTHER,** for any matter covered herein, the special prosecutor shall conduct a full, reasoned, and independent investigation including, but not limited to, (i) gathering and analyzing evidence, (ii) conducting witness interviews, and (iii) reviewing investigative reports, scientific reports, and audio and video recordings;

**FURTHER,** for any matter covered herein, the special prosecutor shall, (i) attend in person, a term or terms of the County or Supreme Court to be held in and for the County of such appropriate jurisdiction consistent with this Order, (ii) appear in person before any grand jury drawn for any term(s) of said court, for the purpose of conducting any and all proceedings, examinations, and inquiries, and (iii) bring any and all criminal actions and proceedings which may be had or taken before said grand jury and other grand juries concerning or relating to any and all alleged unlawful acts as described by this Order;

**FURTHER,** for any matter covered herein, the special prosecutor will provide to me, or my designee, a report on all cases where, (i) the special prosecutor declines to present evidence to a grand jury regarding the death of a civilian as described in this Order, whether in custody or not, allegedly caused by a law enforcement officer, or (ii) the grand jury declines to return an indictment on any charges. The report will include, to the extent possible and lawful, an explanation of that outcome and any recommendations for systemic reform arising from the investigation.

This Executive Order shall continue until modified, suspended or terminated by the Governor.

G I V E N under my hand and the Privy Seal of the State in the City of Albany this eighth day of July in the year two thousand fifteen.

BY THE GOVERNOR

That announcement came at the perfect time because, later that month, to honor and pay tribute to Eric on the one-year anniversary of "that day," I had arranged for events that would last all weekend, from Friday to Sunday. It went into the following Monday when some family members held a march in his name, even paying the subway fares for people to attend if they couldn't afford it themselves.

I held my event on Staten Island, and this was the first time I'd arranged something where I was in charge of everything. I had plenty of people helping, but it was basically up to me to coordinate and oversee everything. The first thing I did was invite anyone and everyone whom I had met over the last year who I thought would be interested in attending. I wanted to show them my appreciation for their support, and I wanted them to have a chance to celebrate Eric's life. Many of them only knew him from the video and from my stories, so I hoped they could come.

I also had the idea to invite as many of the other mothers as I could. I wanted all of them to attend. Through other events, I had seen how powerful we were together, and I hoped that they would be able to come together . . . and they did. There were at least twenty other mothers of victims there, some I'd not even met. When I invited them, I made sure to ask them to tell any other mothers that I hadn't met that they were welcome as well.

It worked. There were several mothers I didn't know, and we embraced each other and exchanged stories, shared experiences, and wiped away some tears. On Friday, after all the moms arrived, we stayed together in a nice New Jersey hotel. It was much easier to fly into Newark, stay there, and then travel to Staten Island. I was able to get sponsors and donors to provide rooms for the mothers and a shuttle service to the events.

I was so grateful for those who donated, and I was proud to be able to do that for the mothers, to treat them to a nice weekend. They deserved that and so much more. Reverend Al Sharpton, Reverend Daughtry, Pastor Bartley, and the Christian Love Baptist Church all helped to make it happen.

On Friday, once everyone was settled, we had a dinner at the Marriott Courtyard and then that evening went to Brooklyn on a bus provided by Pastor Bartley. We arrived at the House of the Lord Church, and Reverend Daughtry spoke to the group and then had an open mic session. He allowed each mother, if they chose to participate, to come up and tell their story. None of the women were rushed or cut off during their time onstage. The reverend told them this was their time and no one would take it away from them. And no one did.

It was such a powerful and emotional night because each strong Black woman stood up in front of the microphone and told her tragic story. The painful words traveled through the room, floating above us and landing like emotional daggers into our hearts and souls. All of them were different, but the message was the same. The pain was the same. The loss was the same. The voices of those ladies took over that night. We were scheduled to go from 7:00 to 9:00 p.m., but we didn't finish until near midnight. The church was understanding and allowed us to stay as long as we needed, sharing our misery. A group formed by our common grief.

I was scheduled to speak at the end, after everyone had finished. I wasn't sure whether I could even get up there at first because those heartbreaking stories were so draining. After they had shared such raw emotions, how could I stand in front of them and talk about the weekend I had planned? Just as I'd been doing all year, I took it one step at a time. I went up to the microphone and looked out at those strong faces, those brave faces, those emotionally drained faces, and I realized that it didn't matter what I said to them. They were not only brave enough to share their own stories but also resilient enough to listen to other tragic stories and show empathy. That was the amazing thing about these mothers. They had endured so much; yet they were somehow able to listen to other stories. Despite their pain, they projected understanding, warmth, and caring. It created a very open atmosphere.

I talked about Eric, about what he was like as a person, about how important he was to me and all of our family, and how much I missed him. Then I thanked everyone for being there and gave them a rundown of the activities I had planned for the weekend. It turned out better than I could have ever imagined. We created a fellowship that day, a fellowship of grieving mothers on a mission.

I didn't know some of the women who attended. Since I had asked the ones I did know to spread the word, that's exactly what they did. There was one mother from Maryland who had established a coalition, and she brought nine other mothers along with her. That was fine by me—the more mothers, the more opportunity to learn from each other. There were others from Georgia, Ohio, New York, and all over. The ones who didn't know each other got to know each other really well during the program on Friday. It was interesting because, with so many people there, they were all at a different stage of grief. It was very new and fresh and raw for some. Then there were others like the mother of Nicholas Heyward, a thirteen-year-old boy who was shot by police in 1994. She had been speaking out for more than twenty years.

It was hard to grasp that she had been doing that for so long and there was still the need. That was the hardest part to come to terms with. This was still happening to our young boys and men in the Black community. And almost all the stories had the same ending—nothing happened to the police officers involved. We grew up thinking that there was fairness and justice in this world, and even when things are now recorded, caught on tape, there is still no change. It's unbelievable.

We had breakfast the next morning; then we went back to the hotel to get ready for the picnic. At 12:30, we rode over to Staten Island, where we had something like a family cookout on steroids, with more than three hundred people showing up. My husband, Ben, cooked fish, we had salad, there was lots of other picnic food, and it was just a fun day to release. Everyone got to interact in an informal setting with no pressures and no social agenda. The only requirement was to relax. It was like a big family—a day of freedom. We even made up funny names for smoothies, like a Legacy Fusion named after Eric's youngest child. There was, of course, one named after Eric as well. It was nice to just let loose and not be so serious.

Despite the levity and fun that we were having, we were never too far from the reality of the tragic bond among us. I heard stories that I'd never heard before. Some involved small children. I learned from that event that when I meet a new mother, I embrace her, but I never ask for her story. I let her tell it if she wants to, but I never ask because I know what I am going to hear. I know it will be tragic.

On Sunday, we went to Christian Love Baptist Church in Irvington, New Jersey, and then to the New Hope Baptist Church for services. They were nice services, and we felt like we all had a lot to pray for and pray about. Then I thanked everyone for coming, my old friends and the new ones I'd made. I also checked to make sure everyone got home safely.

I was proud that I was able to pull that off. I was so grateful for all the help and support I had, but, more important, I was indebted to the women who attended and shared their stories and their strength and their wisdom. It was the perfect way to remember my son and to celebrate the first positive news we'd received after so many disappointments. I decided to accentuate the positive and focus on the good things that happened that month and the new friendships I'd made at the picnic.

To my surprise, as our picnic was ending the DJ played a soul song from the 1970s, and everyone started dancing. That was so amazing and just felt so good, and it was all in Eric's memory. The fun and the seriousness and the food and the music and the fellowship all mixed together seemed like the perfect way to honor my son.

The song that the DJ played was called "I'll Always Love My Mama."

# Chapter 7

○

# The Royal Treatment

Healing begins where the wound was made.
—Alice Walker

IN THE LAST FOUR MONTHS OF 2015, I met several women who would become very important in my life. It started in September when I was contacted and asked to go to Chicago to meet Hillary Clinton. I suppose she had heard about us mothers and our fledgling group of activists. I was excited to meet her because everyone knew she was running for president on the Democratic ticket against Bernie Sanders. I felt so blessed that she was asking me to meet with her.

It still astounded me that I was getting calls from people like her who traveled in much different circles than I could ever imagine. I was learning that along with this activism there are some highs, some successes, and many more lows. Trying to effect change is never easy and never fast—that's what I was learning. Getting that morsel of success from the state of New York took a lot of work by a lot of people. And even that still didn't guarantee anything, but it was a start. You take those wins where you can get them, I was learning.

There were lots of those ups and downs, and that roller coaster of emotions was just something that you had to get used to. I think that's why many people who get involved with being active in the community give up after a little while. It's just too hard and too *defeating* to keep hearing "no." I'm from Brooklyn, and I was raised to stand tough when things got difficult. I had no intention of giving up at this point. Granted, in the beginning there were some moments when I allowed those thoughts to dance around in my head, especially as I stood out in the rain or snow trying to hand information to people who didn't want it.

Yet I didn't give up. One thing that I figured out was that just because we heard "no" didn't mean it was always going to be like that. It just meant "no" for the moment. A lot of people, maybe even Cynthia and the others at NAN, probably thought I would say, "OK, this is enough for me," and I would go away, stop pressing for change, stop using whatever platform I had to call folks out when they were talking foolish. I wasn't about to do that, and I think when people kept seeing me show up at events and saw me on TV or in the newspaper whenever there was an announcement related to police violence or brutality, it kept reminding people that I was still there. I was not going anywhere. Since neither of my sons could be there, this was my responsibility, and I was taking it very seriously.

Yes, I might be a quiet grandmother without a big bank account or high-powered friends, but one of those factors was definitely changing. I was meeting some important people, and they were listening to me. To me! I felt like with each new meeting, I was connecting with someone who might be able to help. I could just imagine what Eric and even Emery would have thought of me at the Prince concert, or meeting JAY-Z or Hillary. They would have been very excited about that.

On September 29, I was flown to Chicago, and there were maybe twelve other mothers there. They brought us together in a private room at a Black-owned restaurant in the heart of the city. As we gathered and sat down, we all looked at each other with stunned expressions. I had met most of the mothers, but there were a couple whom I didn't know, so we made our introductions. There wasn't a whole lot of talk, though. It was almost like we were reverent. I think they were surprised to be there too. Just yesterday, I was in my living room talking to my husband, and today I was meeting Hillary

Clinton. If I thought about it too much, it was just a lot to process, and I wanted to stay focused. I wanted to hear what she had to say.

Then the door swung open, and there she was. Hillary Clinton came in with a couple of people from her team and greeted us immediately. There was no press and no grandstanding. She talked to us about her mission and her ideas, and it was very heartfelt. She said that she had seen each of us in the press and was aware of what we were trying to do. She found our causes very noble and very necessary. She thought we might be able to help each other.

She talked to us as a mother, a protector, someone who wanted the best for future generations. That's what we were all there for. Of course, we wanted justice for the deaths of our children and would never stop fighting for that, but the fact was that they were gone, and we couldn't do anything to bring them back. What we were doing was for all of the others in harm's way, those who felt threatened and intimidated and treated as less than they deserved. That was the big picture for all of us. If we could turn our tragedies into something that helped another innocent person, regardless of race, then, as mothers, that's what we knew in our hearts was right.

Hillary proposed that we join her campaign in 2016, as we were able, and talk to people at her events. That would give us more exposure and a chance to talk to more people about our mission. I was impressed that she had reached out to us, because none of the other candidates did that and she didn't have to, but she did. During that meeting she really listened to us. She focused on each one of the mothers and talked to us directly as individuals, taking notes herself on a small pad.

It gave me a new insight into what a politician could be. I'd already met and worked with several at the state and even national level trying to get a fair trial for my son, so I was somewhat familiar with how they operated. I know they were all doing their jobs, but I also knew there is a lot of deal making and agreements of this for that in order to get things done. I just didn't feel like some politicians I had met were in it for the right reasons. It felt like they wanted something, whether it was to be in the limelight or to get attention for their legislation so that they could take credit, or to be associated with a "mother" to help soften their image and make them more relatable.

Some people think that just because I'm not very vocal, I might not be in tune with things that are going on or that people are taking advantage of me. Believe me, as a mother who has raised many children, especially through those teen years, I know how to read people, and I know what is going on even if someone doesn't tell me about it. And just because I don't say everything that I'm thinking all the time, the way some folks do, that doesn't mean I'm not aware. Believe me, Gwen Carr is woke!

After meeting so many different people on this journey, I've become a pretty good judge of character, and to me, Hillary came across as very sincere and very understanding about the situations and struggles that we had endured. I think the thing that really clicked was that she understood that our maternal instincts are what pushed us to continue, what gave us the strength to keep going and work nonstop to get justice for our loved ones. She had true empathy and compassion, and I can tell you that's not easy to find or easy to convey, especially from someone in a position of power. She didn't talk down to us, and she wasn't dismissive or anything like that. She truly listened, and that felt good.

As we left that meeting, she asked us to think about joining her in her mission to change the country for the better. It felt like a good collaboration between the potential first female president of the country and a group of women who were being collectively referred to as "The Mothers of the Movement," which referred to the Black Lives Matter movement that was becoming more mainstream after so many Black deaths at the hands of law enforcement. Hillary stressed that it was up to each of us individually to decide whether this was right for us and whether we felt comfortable supporting her.

I left that meeting and went home once again feeling energized and encouraged. I had gone from marching down the street in the hot sun to meeting with the woman who was running for president of the United States. It was kind of unbelievable that these types of opportunities continued to come up. Each time I received an invitation like that I was honored by it.

Cynthia Davis was proud of how far I'd come. She told me, "My first impression of you was a person who had just lost a son. You looked like a brokenhearted mother." She said that she respected the fact that while I was angry about what happened to my son, I wasn't bitter or negative toward people, and I always focused on nonviolent solutions. She said that, as many years as she had been working in the community, she was surprised at how well I was handling not only Eric's death but all that had happened since then, the good and the bad.

Cynthia taught me that it is OK to disrupt the status quo and shake up business as usual; in fact, she encouraged it. She took me out every Tuesday and Thursday to protest and raise awareness, and I did it because I could see the big picture. I never expected it to get this big, like meeting Hillary, but I hoped that I was making a difference. During those first protests, it was sometimes just Cynthia and me, and she was always patient and encouraging. We stuck with it, and soon others were joining, and our group got bigger each day. That's where the momentum started, and this meeting gave me the feeling that things were going to a whole new level. Cynthia kept reminding me that people really respond to me and she could tell I was reaching them with my story. That encouragement helped to keep me going.

Fresh off the meeting with Hillary Clinton, I attended my second Congressional Black Caucus forum, and I met many people who became very important to me and my mission. During the conference, I was at the criminal justice seminar headed by Congresswoman Maxine Waters. I was there with Ben, and at the end of the event Congresswoman Waters introduced me to the attendees. There was a woman sitting behind us, and after the presentation she came up, introduced herself, and gave us her condolences. Then she handed me a card that read "Why Tommy?" and it had her name on it—Nadine "Nadia" Fischer. She is CEO of the Why Tommy Initiative, and she is an advocate for the wrongfully convicted and a supporter of LGBT rights.

After the convention, I was helping raise money for the Million Man March that was coming up. So I sent Nadia Fischer an email and asked her whether she would like to donate so that I could get a group of mothers together to attend the march. I wanted to organize transportation and to make it easier for them to attend. I had learned from Cynthia that getting people to show up was the first step of activism. And the best way to do that is to make it as easy as possible. That way, you remove one roadblock. One of the first things someone will say is that they don't have a way to get there. If you remove that issue from the equation, how can they say no?

I contacted a lot of people and requested their support with time, a monetary donation, or both. I was learning fast that once you ask for money, people are often quick to shut you out or they go dark, totally ignoring you. Some people were kind enough to say either that they would or that they were not in a position to do so, but many just did not respond. However, Nadia was one of the gracious people who donated, and that meant a lot to me. She even knew someone in Washington, DC, whom she convinced to help drive us around once we were in the city. That really impressed me.

I knew that she had her own foundation, and I was trying to get the Eric Garner Foundation off the ground but found it difficult to manage. With all of my other growing responsibilities, it was just too much. So, I called her, and we talked for more than an hour. We really hit it off, and I could tell that she knew what she was doing and that she was good at it. I asked her whether she would consider being the executive director of what is now called the ERIC Foundation—Eliminating Racism and Inequality Collectively. She agreed to help temporarily, but her main focus was on public relations, and she offered to be my publicist because that was how she thought she could best help get the word out about Eric and the foundation. We talked a little about strategy and how she could help, and how maybe I could help her. I told her that the biggest event I had was the annual commemoration on the anniversary of Eric's death. I told her what it was like and how much work it had been for me to arrange. She said she could definitely help with that and would be willing to handle the next one if everything worked out between us.

That December, I was contacted about a secret project in New Orleans. I wasn't given a lot of information at first, and I was apprehensive. Since my time in the public eye, I'd had my share of strange phone calls and random people either saying things that weren't very nice or trying to get me involved with some type of event that didn't seem right for me. The fact that I was getting more requests each day made it difficult for me to feel like I was properly vetting them. I certainly didn't want to let any important, crucial opportunities slip by, but I also did not want to get derailed by an event that was not a good fit. That is not as easy as it sounds because when someone wants you to do something, they make it sound as exciting as they can. That's why I was glad that Nadia was coming on board to help me. I needed it.

For this secret project, after I said that I needed more information in order to make a decision, I was told that Beyoncé wanted me and some of the other mothers for a project in New Orleans. I later found out that she was filming a short movie that would go along with her *Lemonade* album and that she wanted us in the video. We weren't told much at all—just to show up and the production people would do the rest. The only thing they asked was that we bring a large photo of the child who had been taken from us. When I got there, I found out that Sybrina Fulton, Wanda Johnson, and Lezley McSpadden were also going to be in the project. We are in a couple of scenes of the video, and it's very powerful. The most impactful scene is where we are each shown, individually, sitting in an antique chair and holding our child's photo in front of us.

It was exciting on a pure fantasy level because we had our own trailers and makeup people and wardrobe. It felt nice to be treated like that, and we enjoyed the experience. It was also interesting to see how it all came together with the filming and staging and everything that was involved. I had already met Beyoncé at the Prince concert, so it was exciting to see her again. The most important thing of all was that she was using her incredible star power to shine a light on what we were doing and what we had gone through. The video was released a couple of months later, but we were under strict orders not to mention it to anyone because it was one of her secret projects, and part of the appeal was the element of surprise. I was very appreciative of the opportunity and the exposure, so not talking about it was not an issue for me. That was my specialty.

It was nice to get that star treatment and be made to feel like we were important, even though it was temporary. Of course, I didn't take it too seriously or let it go to my head because I was so grateful just to have that opportunity. I think that's why a lot of people relate to me and the other mothers; they can see that it's not about us. It's almost like childbirth all over again. We are using our bodies as a vessel to deliver the message of our children. It's not about us—it's about them.

During childbirth, what everyone sees, the visual image, is a woman with a baby inside. While her health is of concern, the focus is on the child growing inside her. When that child is born, there is even more attention on the little one. As mothers, we are important, of course, but we all know that we are sacrificing ourselves for our children. That's what we do. We sacrifice our time, our emotions, and our bodies.

Making appearances and doing things like the Beyoncé video reminded me that I was the messenger, but the message was my son and how he was no longer able to speak for himself. When Eric was a baby and couldn't yet speak, I spoke for him. I interpreted what he was thinking and feeling and translated that for everyone else. He was a part of me, and I understood every essence of him. I knew that I'd always be there for him to support and protect him as best I could.

Being in the public eye and getting so much attention could be a distraction if I allowed that to happen. It would be easy to get caught up in meeting the celebrities and feeling like it was all about me. I think it's natural for people to internalize that attention, and I know it's easy to let it get out of control. I've seen others who have lost their way, forgetting their true mission because they enjoyed the spotlight a little too much. They forgot the whole reason why it began in the first place. Of course, I never judged them or took that away from them; I just knew that I needed to stay focused and grounded.

Another concern I had was that I was deserting my family. My whole life is them and being with everyone. Leaving them to take trips to Chicago and New Orleans and Washington, DC, became more and more frequent. Ben was retired and joined me occasionally, but usually he stayed home. He understood what I had to do. He had always been supportive, but still I worried that maybe this was taking over my life.

While Eric's death at the hands police will always be important to me, I did have to think about everyone else too. Isn't that just like a mother? No matter what we are called to do, we worry that we aren't doing enough, or that we are doing too much. I guess that's just part of God's plan. It's up to us to hold it down, especially in the Black community with the high number of fatherless homes.

So that did concern me. I wanted to make sure I continued to spend time with Ben and Ellisha and my grandchildren. My schedule was getting busier by the day, and I had to come up with some kind of plan. Bringing Nadia aboard would definitely help, but was it enough?

While there were plenty of people willing to give advice about what is involved with activism, one size does not fit all. I was learning that I had to find my own way and decide what worked best for me. I would take advice and guidance from others, but if something didn't feel like it was working, or I didn't feel good about what I was doing, then I knew that wasn't for me. That's where I started learning to trust my instincts as a woman and a mother. I did the same when the children were little. I took advice from others, I observed what worked for them, and then I did things the way that fit best for me and my situation.

I suppose with activism there are guides and programs that you can follow, but for me I found that because my situation was so unique, there really were no rules. My situation was different from the other mothers too, because of the videos that were viewed millions and millions of times. Eric's death was so visual and impactful that people felt that they had a connection with it and him. We had all been spectators in his death, and I realized that it was so much bigger than me or my family.

There was no way I could control it; I could just try to be the best messenger and representative of my son that I could be. I don't think that is in any activism rulebook. It can't be because it's such an individual journey. With all the requests for my time and energy, I wanted to be smart about it and try to make the most impact possible.

This music video was an amazing opportunity, and I knew that with Beyoncé, it would make a big splash and likely stir up a lot of controversy and conversation. Plus, it was going to reach a lot of young people, not only those who felt victimized but hopefully also those who were considering going into the field of law enforcement. I tried to emphasize during every interview that I was not at all against the police, and never advocated disobedience or violence toward them.

However, I did hope that anyone considering going into that line of work, that young generation just coming up, was doing it for the right reasons. I don't think people go into law enforcement with bad intent at all—exactly the opposite. But hearing the stories I'd heard, somewhere along the way things sometimes went sideways and bad decisions were made. When you're in that line of work, bad decisions can cost people their lives. That's what I wanted to get across, and I wasn't sure everyone understood that.

With the Black Lives Matter movement and other civil rights initiatives, people often go to the extreme and think that we are saying other people *don't* matter. It is just the opposite. I would never be a part of a message like that. We are saying that all people matter but not all people are getting the same treatment and respect. If you don't see how others are treated and don't know about it, it's probably natural to think that everyone is treated fairly and equally. Unfortunately, that's not the case.

The videos that Ramsey and Taisha took really put that front and center, and people got to see with their own eyes what things can be like for some people. That level of awareness and education is so crucial to getting any kind of change. People first need to understand the issues, and then they can help come up with a solution.

So, if me being in a music video or doing another interview on TV would help do that, then that's what I was going to do, and I was going to do it the best way for me. I might not dress perfectly or say just the right things, but I was determined to get my point across and let people know that some of the treatment people have to deal with is not acceptable.

At the end of 2015, I took stock of all that happened to me that year. There had been lots of disappointments, but also some small victories. There had been a lot of press and media events. Some went very well, and others were just a mess. Folks were not organized or there were other issues coming up or I felt the questions were not on point. I realized that going into the new year, I wanted to learn from any mistakes I'd made and build on the momentum I'd had. I was putting all my energy into this mission, this new vocation, this new lifestyle, and I wanted to be smart about it.

I took out a piece of paper and wrote down some of the ups and downs of 2015. I had learned long ago that it helped me to lay everything out on the table and then deal with it, the good and the bad. So I listed the highs—like the special grand jury prosecutor and the amazing fellowship at the cookout celebration in Eric's honor. Another highlight was meeting so many other mothers who were dealing with similar situations. I didn't realize it at the time, but it did help to talk and share with them. It was like we all spoke the same sad language, the language of loss.

I didn't even write down any of the low points. There was no need to dwell on the negative. I knew what I had to do.

# Chapter 8

———————————◯———————————

# Putting Hope in Hillary

For when people get caught up with that which is right, and they are willing to sacrifice for it, there is no stopping point short of victory.

—Martin Luther King Jr.

AFTER FINISHING THE BEYONCÉ VIDEO, I circled back with Nadia to talk about the upcoming year and how I was going to handle everything, especially with Hillary Clinton's campaign ramping up. I had taken my personal assessment of where I was and where I wanted to be. My plan was to start 2016 as organized and informed as possible. I knew things wouldn't be perfect and that I'd probably still mess up sometimes or do things that I wished I hadn't, but that's all part of the journey. I felt confident that Hillary was going to win the Democratic nomination, even though other family members were supporting Bernie Sanders. I just felt like she was the right person for the job, and my number-one priority that year was to do everything I could to make that happen.

Nadia was helpful because she basically acted as a sounding board for me at first. She would tell me how I was doing and guide me as far as which opportunities I should pursue and which I should turn down. Like Sybrina told me, sometimes it's OK to say no to opportunities. Just because someone makes an offer that

doesn't mean you have to take it. Nadia said that she liked the way
I carried myself and agreed that I should use my soft-spoken nature
and calm demeanor to my advantage. Those were my strengths, and
that's what helped people feel at ease with me. It was good to hear
someone provide an objective assessment of how I was doing, because it helped to validate my approach and I knew she was looking
out for my best interests.

It had been difficult doing things on my own. I could ask Cynthia or even Reverend Sharpton or family members for their opinion,
but it felt good to finally have someone there to guide me and keep
me on the right track. Nadia gave me the nickname "Julio." She said
it came from a low-budget TV show similar to *Chico and the Man*.
I didn't know what she was referring to, but I thought it was sweet,
and our friendship was off and running. Before we got started, I
shared with her more insight about Eric so she would understand
what I was doing and why I was doing it. I told her how he loved his
family and his children and fought so hard to try to keep everyone
together. I told her about his sense of humor and shared stories
about him, like how he loved to work the grill at the family barbe-
cues as he told jokes.

To me, it was important that she truly know who my son was
and what he stood for. I wasn't sure what she had heard or what
conclusions she had come to on her own, and I had found that the
best way to level the playing field and make sure everyone was on
the same page was to lay things out at the beginning. If we were
going to be working so closely together, I wanted her to know Eric
and understand him and why I was devoting myself to his memory.
That was crucial.

I would get emotional talking about him, especially with her,
because I knew that she had done a lot of work with young Black
men who were incarcerated. She had already heard countless stories, and she knew like I did that behind each of those stories was
a son and brother and father, a real human being. Those men were
more than statistics or stereotypes; they were real people with real
families. She knew what the struggle was like and how unfair the
system could be. I wanted her to understand that if we were working

together, everything that I did, every opportunity I accepted, was in honor of my son.

We didn't have too much time to strategize because Hillary's campaign was kicking into high gear, so if I wanted to be a part of it, I had to jump right in, and that's what I did. One of the first events was on February 23, 2016, in Columbia, South Carolina. I was there with Sybrina, Lucy McBath, Geneva Reed-Veal, and even Gabby Giffords and her husband, Mark Kelly. We were at Central Baptist Church, and Hillary was speaking about how gun violence was tearing apart our communities. Sybrina was one of the featured speakers because of the horrible tragedy that took her son Trayvon's life.

It was a real whirlwind keeping up with that pace. We went from city to city, traveling with the campaign and making speeches and meeting people along the way. It was an unforgettable experience, and I met so many amazing voters. There were lots of dignitaries, but also plenty of regular folks too. They were my favorites because they often shared their own stories, and I knew that no matter where we lived or where we were from, we were all part of the same human experience. They often shared with me their own tragic reality, stories about children who had been the victims of senseless violence. That hit home for me, and I understood their pain. I also understood that we all just wanted it to stop. So I continued to share my story with all of them.

The interesting thing was that I never got tired of telling it. Sometimes when you tell a story too many times it gets old and repetitive, but that was not the case with me and my Eric. It was almost like it had its own life and I was just a small part of it, a physical representation of what they had all seen and heard. It was interesting to learn about some of the assumptions people made and the conclusions they had drawn. I was never upset or judgmental. Like Nadia had told me, I stayed on message and focused on sharing because I could actually see the impact it was having.

All across the country, people were relating to me and understanding and sharing their concern and condolences. They all agreed that this was the most important thing I could have done for Eric, and I got lots of encouragement from them. It felt good being out of New York and finding out that so many people felt the same way, that things had gotten out of hand and the police were going too far all across the country. There needed to be some kind of checks-and-balances system. That would only begin when there was better education and more accountability.

I won't say that it was always perfect. I did meet some people who didn't say nice things, or said something based on ignorance, but it was strange because I thought that would upset me. Instead, it only helped to reinforce that my work was not done, that I needed to keep talking and educating people on what was happening in other communities. I realized that almost any time there was a negative it was because someone just didn't understand all the facts. That was one of the problems with social media and those videos.

When something is so public like the video of Eric's death, it's open to interpretation and comments and commentary by all kinds of people. With all the social platforms, people often feel free to share their opinions and ideas, usually without thinking about the families involved. If they realized Eric's mother or stepfather or sister was reading their comments, I wonder how free they would be with their theories and accusations and assumptions.

It was truly exhausting talking to all those people over and over again, but I realized that it was the best way to reach them. Television interviews were great and appearances on CNN and other news programs reached a wide audience, but there was nothing like being face-to-face with a potential voter and explaining my side of things. I could tell when there was a real connection and when they understood what I had been through. I knew they would never truly know what I'd experienced, but I knew that if I could just reach them, touch their soul, and make that connection, I could help to spread the message of my son and how important his life was before he was taken from us.

That gave me a new appreciation for what politicians go through when they are campaigning and talking to so many people. Speaking to large groups is great, but it's those individual connections where you make the most impact. It's just incredibly draining. Not only does it take a lot of physical energy, but, because of Eric's story, it was also emotionally draining. No matter how much I talked about it, it never got any easier. I suppose if I didn't talk about it at all, if I let that day fade away like the morning fog, then it would be easier to handle. I wouldn't have to handle those emotions over and over.

However, that was my sacrifice. That was the price I was willing to pay to help get Hillary elected because I felt in my heart that she would work hard to make changes in our approach to law enforcement in this country. She could come up with a solution that allowed the police departments to do their job but do it responsibly. And when there were mistakes or bad decisions, there would be accountability and consequences. That didn't seem like too much to ask, and when we met in Chicago she gave me her word that she would make that a priority.

I was still trying to wrap my head around the fact that a candidate for the presidency of the United States, and one who had a good chance of winning, was interested in what I had to say and was promising her support. I never imagined that I would be in that position. I didn't like the reason that I had to be there, but I really did appreciate what she was willing to do, how she was willing to put herself on the line to do the right thing.

As we continued to make our way around the country, we spoke in churches, at town hall meetings, rallies, and concerts. I sat on endless panels discussing the importance of accountability, of ending gun violence, and of improving conditions for Black folks, particularly Black men. I talked to many people and stood at so many microphones that I was getting tired of hearing my own voice. Sometimes when I was talking I'd hear myself and think, *Who is she? What is she talking about?* Then I'd realize it was me. It was like an out-of-body experience as a result of the grueling schedule. I was determined to see it through and show up to every event that I was asked to attend, but I can tell you it was exhausting.

In addition to the in-person appearances, I went on local and national TV programs to talk about why I was supporting Hillary Clinton for president and how I thought she would be a positive influence on our community. I participated in campaign commercials and discussed how I felt that she was looking out for us and how she was concerned about something very important to me—police reform. Sybrina would often discuss the issue of gun violence prevention, and the other mothers would talk about other "common sense" reform policies.

It was my first time getting involved in a political campaign and there was a learning curve for me, but once I got the hang of it, I think I did a good job. Just like every other opportunity, it was a real learning experience, and it helped for me to see politics at work. I was constantly impressed with how Hillary connected with people and how she handled those who disagreed with her. Despite some of the ugliness that was going on with some of the other candidates, she stayed away from that, and I appreciated it. That was one of the reasons I was proud to be associated with her. She conducted herself in a way that was presidential but also felt real and authentic.

Maybe working this closely with her I was able to see a side that a lot of people did not see, because people often mention how she comes across as cold or aloof. What I experienced was just the opposite. She was surprisingly open and candid with me and everyone she met. Had she conducted herself differently, I probably would not have been so closely associated with her because I found that it was important to align myself with people who I thought were positive and inspiring. I had faced too much disappointment and negativity in my life. At this stage, I was not about to invest time and energy in people who did not have values similar to mine. I just don't have the energy to do it. I've got too much work ahead of me to allow that kind of foolishness into my world.

By June 2016, everyone was talking about how Hillary was the presumptive Democratic presidential nominee, and while it wasn't official yet, we all felt a surge of energy and excitement. It was fulfilling to see that all the hard work was paying off. Keeping up that pace was very difficult, but I promised to do it and I didn't waver from that. We spent most of June on the West Coast going to Los Angeles and other California cities, working hard to ensure that such a large state threw its support behind Hillary as the Democratic nominee. That state would be very important for her to win the nomination.

Being so far from home was not easy, and I did miss everyone, but I also knew how important this campaign was, not only to me but also to the country. I made myself available for any rally or focus group they wanted me to attend. The saving grace for me was having a cell phone because I could keep up with the family and what was going on at home. I would call and give updates on how things were going. Ben would tell me how he had seen me on the news or read about Gwen Carr and the other Mothers of the Movement. Talking to everyone made me homesick, but I stayed the course, intent on fulfilling my commitment to Hillary.

I was learning a lot about the political process. Before that, I'd voted for presidents before, but I'd never been so involved in a campaign at the ground level. I was learning about primaries and polls and town halls. It was a lot to take in, and I did my best to keep up. That campaign energy and enthusiasm helped to keep everyone's spirits up, and with each supporting poll we would get more and more excited about the possibility of having our first female president.

Sometimes, when there was a little downtime or just before I went to sleep at night, I'd think about what it would be like to have a woman running the country. I had already witnessed the transformative power that we had as Mothers of the Movement. I could just imagine what it would be like if a woman, a mother, was making decisions that would affect an entire country and even have a global impact. It was exciting to imagine the possibilities, and it felt like we were so close. I knew Eric would be proud that his mother was out there every day telling people to get out and vote. He would be shocked too, because I'd never done anything like working on a campaign before, but he would have loved it. He was always encouraging me to do things for myself, to enjoy myself and stop worrying so much about the family, especially after the children were grown and on their own.

As a mother, there is not a switch that you can just turn on and off. You can't just stop caring because your child is now an adult. To me, Eric would always be that little boy who brought random friends over for dinner and stuck up for the underdog. Having those memories of him made everything else I did possible. When I needed some inspiration and motivation, I could focus on those times spent around the Christmas tree or the silly jokes he told or the way he and Emery would pick on each other or the way he would try to protect Ellisha. That was the Eric I would always treasure.

That July marked the second anniversary of my son's passing, so, as she had promised, Nadia assisted my daughter Ellisha and others with organizing everything for the remembrance event. I had put the first one on myself, and this time I wanted to really make an impact, a big splash. That way we would get a lot of press, and it would continue my mission to keep Eric's name out there. So I was glad to get a fresh perspective. I was hoping Nadia would be able to help us attract some well-known people to help build a buzz.

When everything came together, the ERIC Garner Way Foundation presented a peace walk, a unity fest, and a day of worship. The peace walk kicked off at 9:00 a.m. on July 16 in Prospect Park in Brooklyn. The unity fest followed the walk, and we arranged for transportation to take folks to the New Hope Baptist Church in Elizabeth, New Jersey. At the unity fest, we had speakers like Al Sharpton, radio personality Doug Oliver, and minister Kirsten John Foy.

The highlight was when Nadia was able to arrange a video message from none other than Beyoncé. Apparently, she was on the European leg of her *Lemonade* tour, but despite that she had contacted Nadia to find out whether there was anything she could do for the event since we had worked together on the video and she knew about the anniversary of Eric's death. She sent a representative named Bill to help coordinate everything. He made sure to get JAY-Z's mother there, and he arranged for all the audiovisual technology needed. Of course, they wanted to make sure everything was on point.

It was amazing that she was able to take time out of her touring schedule to do a live greeting like that. She was a beautiful black-and-white image on a huge monitor as she delivered an emotional and powerful message of support for Eric and for all that I was doing in his name. She went out of her way to send us that message, and it was so appreciated. She continued to amaze me with all that she did to help us with our mission.

In addition, Nadia made sure that we communicated our message at the event and on our flyers. We had the following printed up to share with attendees:

## ERIC: Eliminating Racism and Inequality Collectively

ERIC, also known as the Garner Way Foundation, was established to empower others with the knowledge and awareness of the ongoing crisis we face continuously, which is racism and injustice. Our goal is to arm those in need with educational tools that will combat these unfortunate situations when necessary.

### Our Story

This is in dedication, memory, and protest of the wrongful choking death of Eric Garner, forty-three years old, father of five children, who on July 17, 2014, was put into a chokehold after apparently breaking up a fight outside a local storefront in Staten Island, New York. Five New York police officers surrounded him, and one of the police officers put him in a chokehold, then forced him onto the ground with the chokehold still applied around his neck. Eric Garner shouted out "I can't breathe" eleven times. As a result, Eric Garner died shortly thereafter. A Staten Island Grand Jury has voted not to indict the New York police officer in the killing of Eric Garner, which emotionally disturbs the nation.

Later that month I was invited to attend the New York Civil Liberties Union (NYCLU) benefit called "Broadway Stands Up for Freedom." The event is held each year by the NYCLU, which is a group that has been around since 1951 to defend people's rights as indicated in the U.S. Constitution. The group helps to fight for freedom of speech, equality, and due process of law for all New York citizens. As with all events, I had learned to do my research before agreeing to anything.

According to the NYCLU website:

When the NYCLU was founded, civil liberties were under siege. McCarthyism was in full swing and blacklisting and loyalty oaths were the norm. Government censorship of books and magazines was common, and abortion was a crime. Blacks, Latinos and other people of color were subjected to discrimination in education, housing and employment. Gay, lesbian, bisexual and transgender New Yorkers lived in fear of exposure. Students were virtually without rights. The NYCLU has led the way and helped to create a more open, just and equitable society. The NYCLU fights for civil liberties and civil rights through a multi-layered program of litigation, advocacy, public education and community organizing. We represent ordinary people who have experienced injustice and have decided to fight back. Our clients are men and women, rich and poor, gay and straight, black, white and brown, young and old, religious and atheist, able-bodied and living with a disability, citizens and immigrants. When we vindicate their rights, all New Yorkers benefit.

The event is a big deal every year in New York, and I thought it would be good exposure. Every time I showed up at something, people would recognize me and my highlighted curls. Then they would remember that I am Eric Garner's mother, so I thought that any of those high-profile events were a good way to keep his name out in the public's mind because I know that it's easy for a news story to fade away. I didn't want that to happen, so I agreed to attend the event.

Of course, it was star studded, with lots of Broadway performers, local dignitaries, and other important folks. It was a full program where they discussed the importance of fighting for the rights of everyone and how important it is to speak out and get involved. I could honestly say that I was about as involved as anyone could get, and I agreed that it was very empowering.

Nadia and I discussed these opportunities when they came up because while I did want to make sure that I kept Eric's name out there and in people's mouths, I started to worry that I might be getting too much exposure. Was there such a thing? I hadn't thought of that before, but when I saw my pictures online, on the red carpet, I started to wonder whether people were going to get tired of me. Did I have an expiration date, a shelf life for my public appearances? Up to that point, I said "yes" as much as possible, but Nadia pointed out that since I was now helping to represent Hillary's presidential campaign, I did need to keep that in mind.

We didn't come up with any hard and fast rules, but we decided that we did need to be cautious and vigilant about future appearances. I had to remember that now it was not just about Eric or me but also about the possible next president. I wanted to make sure that whatever I did, it was keeping in line with the principles and values that I'd heard her share from the road. It was important to me that if I was going to lend my name (and, more important, my time) to something, then I was going to be fully committed to it. I wasn't going to take my commitment lightly.

At the end of the day, the only thing I really have is my name and my reputation, so they have to be something I protect. I talked before about how there is no activism rulebook that works for everyone, and that goes for being in the public eye as well. Because of the way I was known, I wanted to be careful that I was doing things the right way—I just had to figure out what that was. Having Nadia along for the ride helped me make more informed choices when it came to public appearances and media events.

She was great at evaluating a request, vetting it, and providing me with her thoughts on whether it was something we should pursue. That was important to me because, with all the demands on my time, I had less and less of it to give. I also still wanted to make time for Ben and my family and our get-togethers. That was impossible when I was on the road, so when I had a little bit of downtime I wanted to be careful about what I took on.

After being a part of that campaign, it was easy to get caught up in that momentum and excitement and just immediately agree to do something. I just never imagined in a million years that I would be worrying about which red carpet events to attend and what speaking engagement I should accept. At this stage of my life, it was as much of a surprise to me as anyone else. I guess when you are presented with something like what happened to Eric, you have to decide at that moment how you are going to respond. Lots of family members handled things differently, and that's OK. We all have to do what feels right for us. I just couldn't wait until we got to the election and Hillary won the presidency, but first she had to clinch the nomination.

The Democratic National Convention was held from July 25 to 28, 2016, in Philadelphia, Pennsylvania. It was there that Hillary Clinton, along with her vice presidential running mate Tim Kaine, was chosen as the official Democratic nominee for president. The convention included several days of panels and presentations. Elizabeth Warren was the keynote speaker, and there were countless others in attendance, including Barack and Michelle Obama, Bill Clinton, Bernie Sanders, Cory Booker, Nancy Pelosi, Harry Reid, and Joe Biden. There were even folks there like Meryl Streep and Angela Bassett.

The party agreed to focus on several key issues, including financial regulations, criminal justice reform, and important programs like social security and welfare benefits. There was also talk about focusing on strengthening the Affordable Care Act, improving education, and expanding workers' rights. Those all seemed like reasonable, no-nonsense issues, and I couldn't really see how anyone wouldn't want to support them.

It was a bit overwhelming meeting the sheer number of people there. I'd met plenty of important people over the last year or so, but this was at a whole different level. There were so many senators and congresspeople and mayors and celebrities. It was a lot to take in. The programs on the second day focused on fighting for children and families, and I found those especially important.

Several of us were there as part of the Mothers of the Movement. On day two of the convention, we were onstage taking part in a panel discussion. In attendance with me was Maria Hamilton, mother of Dontre Hamilton; Annette Nance-Holt, mother of Blair Holt; Geneva Reed-Veal, mother of Sandra Bland; Lucia McBath, mother of Jordan Davis; Sybrina Fulton, mother of Trayvon Martin; Cleopatra Cowley-Pendleton, mother of Hadiya Pendleton; Wanda Johnson, mother of Oscar Grant; and Lezley McSpadden, mother of Michael Brown. As we walked onstage, people in the audience shouted their support with "Black lives matter!"

By that time, we had traveled all over the country and people had gotten used to seeing us together, a band of mothers representing the effects of police brutality and gun violence on the community. It had gotten to the point where we rarely needed an introduction anymore. Just as the audience shouted out that day, people knew who we were and why we were joined together to spread a message of accountability and responsibility for all people.

The entire convention was a beautiful celebration of the six months we had spent together working so hard for the mission that we all believed in so strongly. It was fun seeing performances by people like Boyz II Men, Alicia Keys, Lenny Kravitz, and Snoop Dogg, but that was just icing on the cake. I knew that the focus was on winning the presidency. I was just so excited that I would see a female U.S. president in my lifetime. I had never even dreamed that was a possibility a few years ago. Of course, I never expected a Black man to do it, either, but I was pleasantly surprised by the amazing eight years when Barack Obama ran the country.

Once again, I met so many people that day that I could barely keep them straight. A poised, well-dressed woman stopped me in the hallway. "Aren't you Gwen Carr?"

"Yes," I answered.

"Hi, I'm April Ryan, White House correspondent for American Urban Radio Networks."

"Nice to meet you."

"Well, we actually met before. I saw you at Hillary Clinton's town hall in Baltimore. I was also at the Prince concert."

"Oh, that concert was wonderful. I'm sorry I didn't remember you. I meet a lot of people and sometimes just can't keep them straight."

She smiled at me. "Oh, that's OK, Mrs. Carr. I'm working on my second book, *At Mama's Knee*, and I wanted to ask you if I could mention you and your case in the book."

"Yes, that would be wonderful. We will take all the attention we can get. I'm hoping that once Hillary is in office, things will really change." I knew that April was becoming more well known as an author and a news commentator, so I was appreciative of anyone who would write about Eric and keep his name out there. When anyone asked a question like that, if they could mention me along with Eric, I was almost emphatic about it. *Yes! Talk about me, talk about him, just keep writing and saying Eric's name until things change.*

On July 28, the last day of the convention, the highlight was Hillary Clinton being introduced by her daughter, Chelsea, and officially accepting the Democratic nomination for president of the United States. It felt amazing that all our hard work was paying off. I had learned so much over the past few months about how politics worked and what it took just to get nominated, much less elected. It was truly overwhelming. It was very fulfilling work, but also emotionally draining.

I was excited when I was contacted by a representative from Beyoncé's team. The album and video had been released a few months back and had taken the country by storm. I knew that she was very popular, and I liked her music, but I just wasn't prepared for how universal it was. I saw and heard about it everywhere I went. Everyone was talking because of course the whole project had been top secret, so when a complete album came from out of nowhere, people were very surprised.

Not only that, but they were also very surprised by the tone of the album and the subject matter. This was following her very polarizing and inspiring performance during the Super Bowl halftime that year, when she performed her single "Formation." Some people perceived the images as having an anti–law enforcement message and a tribute to the Black Panthers. A lot of discussion was going on at that time about the Black Lives Matter movement and the hashtag #BlackLivesMatter. Again, people were taking that to mean that other lives didn't matter, which wasn't the message at all. But it sure made some folks feel a certain type of way.

Her album continued with the same themes, controversial topics like Hurricane Katrina, the treatment of Blacks in America, and the importance of having pride in your heritage. In the song "Forward," the four of us mothers (me, Wanda, Sybrina, and Lezley) are featured with the photos we brought of our children. We had no idea what it would look like when it was completed, so it was very interesting to see how her vision had been realized, not only in the album but also in the video. In addition, the entire video was shown on HBO, so that opened it up to a whole new audience.

It was amazing how many people contacted me to tell me they had seen me and Eric in the video. None of them could believe I was in it because I hadn't said anything. I told them, "I couldn't! I promised Beyoncé I wouldn't say anything. I couldn't disappoint her!" People laughed when I told them that because after it came out there was a lot of talk about how she did that without anyone even knowing it was going on. I guess that is part of the magic of Beyoncé.

Her representative wanted to know whether I could join Beyoncé and some of the other ladies at the 2016 MTV Video Music Awards in New York at Madison Square Garden. Of course, I was excited, and this was yet another event that I got to see through to the end. I had been at the initial filming, and here we were going to an award show. It felt good to follow these opportunities from start to finish. It helped to show that things were happening, and people were talking and questioning things and hopefully thinking about how things could be improved.

I got dressed up for the event and wore a gold gown. Beyoncé was there with a large crew of women from the project, including Sybrina, Wanda, and Lezley, and of course her husband, JAY-Z, and her daughter, Blue Ivy, were there. We walked the red carpet and posed for pictures before being seated in a reserved section with a perfect view of the stage. I couldn't believe the things I had been fortunate enough to take part in.

Now, if I'm being totally honest, I didn't know who a lot of the performers were that night. There were some whom I did recognize and some who seemed familiar, but mostly they were for a different generation and not folks whom I had listened to. That didn't change my excitement level at all, though. I was into the moment and enjoying every minute of it. We were all taking selfies and posing for photos during breaks between the awards and music acts. One thing they don't tell you is that there is a lot of downtime during those shows.

We cheered loudest when Beyoncé took the stage and performed a medley of songs from her album. Watching her do her thing up close was very exciting, and seeing how much of herself she put into her show was truly something to behold. She took home a bunch of awards that night. I had to look up which ones they were because I didn't remember them specifically, but she won Best Female Video for the song "Hold Up," Best Female Video for "Hold Up," and Video of the Year for "Formation." Then the *Lemonade* album won something called the Moonman Award for Breakthrough Long-Form Video.

After the show, Beyoncé came up to me and asked whether we would like to join her and her family for dinner, and of course I said yes! We went down to Little Italy and had the best time. She is such a wonderful human being. Then she continued to bless me by inviting me to join her in Los Angeles, where Quincy Jones was honoring her. It was just amazing how things like that kept happening. I continued to allow those types of gifts to come my way and receive them in the spirit of gratitude and humbleness. I was just so thankful for everything these people did to help keep Eric's name alive.

I didn't have a lot of time to think about those things because I had to be back to work. Now that Hillary was the official Democratic candidate, our schedule was more packed than ever before. In September, Maria Hamilton, Geneva Reed-Veal, and I were at the North Carolina Central University School of Law talking to a large audience about our experiences with the criminal justice system. Everyone there was very warm and receptive to our message. There were many students and faculty along with people in the legal field.

October was filled with more appearances and campaigns. A lot of them were focused in the South and in what they called the battleground states. In Durham, North Carolina, we were at a church and stood behind Hillary with our fists in the air to show our support. There were events in Pennsylvania, Florida, all over the place. In every location in every state, we kept sharing our stories in the hopes of touching people's hearts and helping them to understand who the best choice was to run this country.

My message was always the same: It was imperative that the criminal justice system experience real reform. Our advocacy needed to turn into action. Things needed to be done. I kept stressing that my son's death was ruled a homicide; yet no one was held accountable. How does that happen in this day and age? Every time I emphasize that, people are always amazed. They know the video, but they don't know the whole story. It cuts deep, and it's not a wound that will ever heal—at least not for me.

The press kept saying that we were there to influence the Black vote and help inspire them to go to the polls. That was partially true. We did want them to go to the polls and vote for Hillary, but I didn't just want the Black vote. I wanted *all* votes. One of the problems is that we keep saying this is a Black issue and a Black problem. I was trying to get across to everyone that it's not a Black problem—it's an American problem. If I was just trying to reach Black folks, that would be preaching to the choir.

Believe me when I tell you that Black folks are very familiar with the problems we face daily in society. Dealing with law enforcement and prejudice and inequality and poor treatment is just another day for us. We don't need someone to tell us there is an issue. What we need is to reach other people, those who do not have the same experiences that we do. They likely have no idea what we go through just to shop in a department store without feeling uncomfortable.

People might hear about it and think they understand, but most folks I've talked to said they had no idea that's what it was really like out there in the streets. They couldn't believe that we were not shocked by how Eric was treated in that video. We did not like it, I can promise you that, and it made us angry and upset, but there was one thing we were not, and that was surprised. For a lot of people, that is a way of life and a daily occurrence. The police officers were upset because they got caught. They never expected that video to go soaring out into cyberspace. Never in a million years.

They thought it was just another day when they were flexing their police muscle and making sure the Black men and women in that area were afraid of them. They used fear and intimidation as their weapon, and we were never surprised to hear yet another story about harassment at the hands of police. Each time I met another mother and heard yet another horrible story, my heart sank, and in my head I thought, *Not again*. I mean, seriously, how many times does it have to happen?

So, when people would ask us whether we thought we were reaching the Black voters, I would say that I hoped we were reaching all voters. Motherhood is universal, and it goes beyond race. It's about being treated fairly and humanely, and then having consequences when those basic tenets of human behavior are not followed. It really is not a complicated concept, but I know it gets people upset. First, they don't like to think of police officers as being so cruel and heartless. Al Sharpton's words always ring in my head: "When does your humanity kick in?" Second, they don't want to think people are being treated that way. They might see it in a movie or hear it in the lyrics of a rap song, but they don't want to actually know about it. That makes it too real, and they have to either deal with it or ignore it. Who could live with themselves if they were aware of that horrible behavior and did nothing?

So that's why I protested and campaigned and showed up at every single event. That's why I pushed past my limits and pain as a woman in her golden years who would rather be at home in her recliner. After what I had been through and what I had seen, of course I could never go back to just sitting on the sidelines. I will admit that if Eric hadn't been murdered, I would not be where I am today. I would not have been out on the campaign trail and away from my loved ones. I would likely have been at a family cookout laughing and having a good time and enjoying the company of Eric, Ellisha, and my grandchildren, aunts, uncles, and cousins.

However, I do think that God has a plan, and this is the one for me. I don't know why or what it all means, but I do know that I'm giving this my best shot. I have one life, and these are the cards I've been dealt. I have to play them carefully, and that's what I'm working hard to do. The main thing is that I hope Eric would be proud of what I've done, for him and Emery. There's nothing I can do to bring my sons back, but, as a mother, I have to try to help make a difference. There are others fighting for change too, and many of them are better at it than I am, and they've been doing it for much longer.

I am grateful to those folks, and I realize that I have to do my part. I've been given this experience and this platform, and I'm doing my best to use it for the greater good. If I can turn a tragedy into something positive, then I've done my best. If there's anything I've learned from Hillary, it's that good intentions don't win races or get things accomplished. You have to be out there. You have to show up. Even then there are no guarantees, but you have to try.

I was told that since people recognize me, the way April Ryan did at the CBC, that is what I need to use. I need to be seen and heard, and I need to use that recognition to get people's attention. Once I have their attention, I can share my message and hopefully educate them. Armed with that information and that education, maybe they can take that and educate someone else and pass it along.

One of the things Cynthia Davis taught me was that it's all a long shot and we have to realize that. If it were easy, if it were a slam dunk, it would have been done by now. Getting people to change is not easy. People don't like to face the ugly facts of police brutality and racism. It is not pleasant, and it's not a fun topic. There's no way to put a nice bow on it. It's evil and cruel. There's no getting around that. We need to put on our big girl drawers and deal with it. If I can do it, these folks out here in the audience watching me speak can do it too. That's what I would try to tell them. This isn't meant to be an emotional presentation that generates your sympathy and then you go on to your Pilates or yoga class. It's meant to help you visualize what is happening beyond your half-acre yard and your HOA-maintained neighborhood, because it is happening everywhere.

I won't go into Sybrina's story because that is hers to tell, but Trayvon was in a totally different environment than Eric was, and I think that helped to shed light on the problems with "stand your ground" and neighborhood watch programs and all of that. The lesson is that these issues are universal and can happen anywhere.

It's what we do afterward that matters. Do we just manage our grief, seal it away in a neat package, and bring it out once a year? Or do we try to tell people what is actually going on in places other than where they live?

I'm not sure how successful I was in sharing that message with all the nice people we met on that campaign trail, but no one can say I didn't try. That's for sure. Whenever I could, I focused on how important it was to find solutions to these problems because, if not, it could happen to someone else's loved one, and I did not want that to happen. I didn't want anyone else to have to deal with the pain that I and the other mothers have had to endure.

As one mother to another, that was the most important thing I could communicate. I did not want anyone to have to deal with these issues again. All of us mothers had endured enough pain and hurt and misery for everyone. We would gladly be the last people to ever have experienced those horrible incidents if it meant that no one else would have to suffer. That's what mothers really do—they sacrifice themselves and their comfort for others.

That's what Hillary said was our strength and the message we could share with others. If there was some way we could make changes in the system, it would never be perfect, but it just might save lives and prevent further misery. Being able to turn Eric's tragedy into even the smallest of victories would help to give it more meaning than just the sheer brutality that was foisted upon my son that day. I still can't get over how people can conduct themselves like that and then go home to their families and to their mothers with a clear conscience. How does someone make peace with actions like that? It just astounds me every time I stop to break it down like that.

That's why that campaigning was so challenging. Of course, those red carpet moments and award ceremonies were much easier because I just had to lend my image to the event. I simply had to show up and make sure I was seen so that people would look at me and think, *Oh, yeah, Eric Garner*. That was easy, because I could help keep the awareness up without having to talk about it. On the campaign trail, my job was to relive the event over and over every single day. I had to keep telling it and keep sharing how horrible and dehumanizing it was to see my son treated that way. Losing him was almost more than I could bear.

It felt good when people responded positively and when they came up to commiserate and console me after the programs, but that didn't make it any easier to talk about the worst day of my life time after time after time. However, as I continued, I realized that I was stronger than I'd ever been. It happened gradually, and I didn't realize it at first, but I did get stronger. Before this happened, I wouldn't have imagined that I could even do this, much less keep on doing it, and in front of total strangers!

I will say it did feel good when I looked out into the audience and saw someone connecting with what I was saying. Not necessarily just someone nodding in agreement, but when I really reached someone, when they really understood my pain and my drive and my determination, I could see it register in their concerned face. That's when the switch flipped in my brain. That's when I knew that I was making a difference, and that's why I was there.

The final days leading up to November 8, Election Day, were busier than ever. Hillary was going nonstop, and I was doing all I could to contribute. The entire campaign was energized by the polls that continued to tout Hillary as leading her opponent, often by a large margin. I did let that get me excited, but I also didn't take it for granted. I know enough to realize that people put out things to support how they feel, so just because a poll said she was leading didn't mean that was the time to get comfortable. However, it did feel good to see that we were all making some sort of impact.

By the time November 8 rolled around, I can tell you that Miss Gwen Carr was tired. I'm really not sure how Hillary did it because she, of course, made more speeches, shook more hands, and talked to many more people than I did. Also, she had to withstand all the negativity and pure nastiness sent her way. I have never seen grown folks behave so poorly. The name-calling and backstabbing just went to a level I had never seen, and it was shocking.

I think what really hit home for me was that I couldn't believe people would say those things about a woman they didn't even really know. Over these many months, I had gotten to know her heart, and it was just so sad that others didn't get to see that. She was stoic and determined and resilient, more so than anyone else I've ever seen before. I thought I could see it wearing on her, but that might have been my imagination because she definitely didn't show it.

It may have been better if she had. I know she wanted to demonstrate that she could be strong in the face of any adversity, and she was, but I kept thinking that she should use her gender and her role as a mother to her advantage. She didn't have to be like the men who were running. The entire appeal of her was that she was different, she was empathetic, she was a mother. I had learned that on the campaign trail, that I needed to embrace my role and use that to help deliver my message. I couldn't come across angry or like some other activists might. In my situation, that wouldn't have worked. Connecting with folks on a personal level and as a concerned mother seemed to work for me.

For a minute, I thought that might have been the way Hillary could have handled it. I know that if a candidate came across like that to me, it would be appealing. We all know how mothers are the complete package. We are caring and compassionate and loving, but if you threaten us or our family, we will come at you with a force like you've never seen.

Maybe all that campaigning went right to my head because here I was thinking that I could give Hillary Clinton advice on how to run for president! It wasn't really that. I knew that she was doing things the way she saw fit, and the way she handled that criticism really impressed me. As part of being in the public, I'd learned not to take everything that people said and did too personally. Many times it was out of anger or plain ignorance. The best thing to do was to try to educate folks so they had a better understanding. Anger and hostility was not the way to get things done. No one ever gets any-where through sheer anger and bad behavior, or at least that's what I thought until that fateful day when the election results started rolling in.

I was at the Javits Center in Manhattan that night along with the other Mothers of the Movement. In addition, Nadia was there, along with my family and many politicians and celebrities like New York governor Andrew Cuomo, Bill de Blasio, Chuck Schumer, Cher, and Katy Perry, and of course Al Sharpton was there to support. Based on the positive poll numbers and early results that rolled in, everyone was feeling very good at the beginning of the evening. That huge facility was beautifully decorated in posters and photos and "I'm with her" banners; it was just breathtaking and felt very patriotic. Huge monitors played campaign commercials and videos, including the ones we had done.

It was a little strange to see myself up on that huge screen, but it reminded me of the campaign and all that we had done and that made me smile. Hearing the commercials with the positive messages and uplifting themes kept our spirits up. Then we began watching the news commentary and the second-by-second breakdown of everything that happened that night. They talked about polls that had closed, the ones about to close, and the ones that would later close, and they dissected every single aspect of the process and more. I had never been so involved in a campaign and had no idea how intense things could get, especially when the results were being tabulated.

I keep using a roller coaster as an example for a lot of the up-and-down moments I experienced, but this was different. We had those early highs when results came in for Hillary, but then it went downhill and there was no coming back. With a roller coaster, you go up, come down, and then level out with a final sense of euphoria at the end. There was no euphoria that night for us. With each state that came in for the other candidate, I could just feel that things were not going to turn out as we had all hoped and prayed and worked so hard for.

It looked so grim that I truly wanted to just leave, go home, and get in bed. But that was the old Gwen talking. I don't do that anymore. It's not to say that I don't want to and that the thought doesn't enter my mind at times. I just have to stop and remember that it won't solve anything. I had been through so many difficult times that now, finally, I was learning how to handle things without letting the devil get his hands on my spirit. It was about staying focused and reminding myself that if I allowed that hopeless feeling into my heart, it was all over for me. I would not be able to continue my mission to share Eric's story. There was too much at stake to allow those old ways to come back.

Times like that, difficult times when things were not going as planned, are what the devil preys on. He searches for that weakness because he knows that means we are not as vigilant, those of us who are susceptible to depression. So no matter how sad I was at the huge red states that were flashing on the big screen, I was determined not to run away. I would face this, figure out a way to process it, and move on with my mission. I had made that promise to Eric, and I wasn't going to let a bully stop me. I had come too far to let that happen.

That was one of the toughest nights of my life because it meant so much not only to me but also to Eric. I saw Hillary as basically our last hope for any kind of reform for law enforcement across the country, and possibly some justice for Eric's murder. Watching that slip away was so defeating and disheartening. I had laid it all out on that campaign trail. I shared all I could, and I tried to connect with as many people as possible. Losing that election felt like I was failing, and that was not a feeling that I liked. It just amazed me that people were willing to support hate. Of course, we later found out that there might have been other factors meddling with the results, but I don't know a lot about that.

What I do know is that it really seemed like once again, like so many times in our history, Black people and those who are oppressed by the system were not getting the representation that they needed. It saddened me that I wasn't even more upset, because the fact of the matter was that people like me are used to disappointment. We are used to being treated like we are not equal and do not have the same value as people who do not look like us. Disappointment is a sad and unfortunate part of our heritage.

The one thing that always holds true, just as it has done in Selma, and at the lunch counters, and on buses, and atop flagpoles, is that we take that disappointment, and it might slow us down for a minute, but we channel it. We have the benefit of one thing that we never wanted: We have so much experience dealing with bad news and tragedy that we have learned we can't let it stop us. We use it as fuel to keep going and keep fighting. That's what I realized I needed to do after that horrible night on November 8, 2016.

I had to take what we were given and use it to continue my mission. There had to be some way to continue fighting. If it couldn't be with Hillary, I just needed to figure out what else could be done. I had learned a lot about politics over the past year, but there was a lot I did not know. I still had hope there was something that could be done.

That's one of the key elements of this crazy world of activism. You have to be passionate to be successful. You have to feel the mission in your heart, and it has to be a part of your spirit, but the trick is that you can't let the defeats stop you. That was much easier to say than do, but to be effective you have to learn how to process those setbacks and then keep on pushing forward. People would love it if, at the first sign of true adversity, we just gave up. That won't work. It is not easy to move past the hurt after putting so much of yourself into something so close to your heart, but you just have to find a way to do that. That's what I did.

After the event at the Javits Center, my first step was to recharge. I was careful not to get too comfortable, but I did allow myself to step back for a minute and get myself together. I also gave myself permission to be sad and disappointed. I had earned the right to do that, and it was important for a couple of reasons. Spending time with family and reflecting on the past year allowed me to really understand how everything had played out. I took that time to just breathe.

I also wanted to make sure that I was in touch with what that moment felt like. I wanted to always remember that defeat because, as I progressed on my journey, I wanted to use that to stay motivated. That was not a feeling I wanted to go through again, so using it as motivation could get me through some of the other difficulties I would likely face. No matter how hurtful and painful that election was, it didn't compare to the horrific things I had already been through. This wasn't about to stop me.

What I realized, and something that Nadia pointed out, was that since President Barack Obama would be leaving office in couple of months, we needed to do whatever we could before the entire administration at the White House changed over. She was right about that, and so we got to work. She helped the family draft a letter to Attorney General Loretta Lynch asking her to ensure that the U.S. Justice Department review Eric's case and do it quickly.

We had a press conference right after the election results, and it was attended by family members, community leaders, and local politicians supportive of our mission. It was our hope that there would be some form of federal indictment since the state of New York had failed in its mission to bring anyone to justice for killing my son. Later that month, after we had made the official announcement, we brought out a lot of home-cooked food to serve the hungry since it was Thanksgiving. We wanted to make that event a positive one where we not only asked for help from the U.S. Justice Department but also provided help to others by feeding hungry local people. Events like that were my favorite because we asked for something but gave something at the same time.

We were not about just asking and taking, we wanted to give as well. We wanted to turn our negatives to positives. Taking those defeats and turning them around was the best way to continue our mission. So we drafted a letter and sent it to the current attorney general of the United States. That was really our last legal option to get some type of justice for Eric, and we held on to it. It was our plan to fully explore whatever we could. That is where Al Sharpton and NAN really helped, because they had been doing this for so long they knew how to navigate within the system.

That is what we had to do—use the system to try to get justice. Of course, we had to follow protocol and work within the established framework, but I still continued to share my story, in my own way, to try to connect with people and get their help. That's what I hoped Loretta Lynch would do. She was in a position where she could help us move forward, and I hoped as a woman that she could understand what I was going through and have some compassion.

I know that things have to follow an established pattern, but I also know that powerful people can make things happen when they really want to. I wanted Loretta Lynch to understand how important this was to use. We needed her help and we needed it quickly, before the new administration took office and brought in new department personnel. Then we would be back to square one. That was a scary proposition because, like the rest of the country and the world, we had no idea what the incoming administration had in store.

Here's the letter I submitted from my heart:

U.S. Department of Justice
950 Pennsylvania Avenue, N
Washington, DC 20530-0001
Attention: Attorney General Loretta Lynch
RE: Justice for Eric Garner—A Mother's Cry

Dear Attorney General Lynch:

You are my last hope; I pray you hear my cry.

My son Eric laid under my heartbeat for 9 months and I continued to nurture him until his last breath as an adult. For the past 2 years I have been searching for understanding as to why this tragedy found me and the answer has yet to become clear. Instead, I'm meeting mothers whose tragedies are similar to my own. As the tears fall from my eyes, my body grows weak. But, I still find the strength to put my arms around these mothers. The look of despair in their eyes mirrors my own and their tears become my tears. Attorney General Lynch, they look to me for hope, just as I am to you.

Visualize my cry for help after I read my son's autopsy report. It said that the cause of his death was a "homicide"—this means "a deliberate and unlawful killing of a person by another." Imagine my tears as I watched the video of my son's last moments breathing. Yes, the world heard my son say eleven times, "I can't breathe." But he also said, "this stops today." Does it?

Despite the recent political upset, I ask that your intervention as the Attorney General of the United States of America be the light of hope for our country by setting the precedent that these injustices will not be tolerated and that those responsible must held accountable. Please hear my cry, don't allow my son's words and our tears to be in vain.

I've been living in a nightmare and crying for over 2 years and I'm ready to awake to peace.

Respectfully,

Gwen Carr
Mother of Eric Garner

# Chapter 9

―――――――――○―――――――――

# Mother to Mother

The cost of liberty is less than the price of repression.

—W. E. B. Du Bois

I THOUGHT I HAD SEEN SOME dark days in my life, but nothing compared to January 2017 when my president, Barack Obama, left office and the newly elected one moved in. I was glad there weren't many people to show up for the inauguration because I didn't blame them. It was not easy to see our hope walk out those doors. Hillary's defeat was very hard to accept, but, just like with the video of Eric, actually seeing it happen made it all very real. My plans for a compassionate administration that would give our case a fair chance seemed to be evaporating before my eyes. While I had learned long ago not to make assumptions about folks, from what I had seen and heard so far, I didn't have a lot of confidence that we would get the help we needed from the new White House resident.

The previous administration left without making any advances in Eric's case. We found out that if the attorney general got involved, it would be a conflict of interest, so there wasn't much they could do. We were advised to be patient and let the justice system work. That sure didn't give me a lot of confidence.

I wasn't following a roadmap on this journey, so I never knew what twists and turns awaited me. It was my hope that we would one day soon get some justice for Eric's death. Then I'd figure out what to do next. If that did happen and those involved were forced to take responsibility, what then? What would I do? Would I continue this path of activism? I wasn't really sure. It could all just stop. I hadn't mapped out a plan of what-ifs (if this happened, I would respond in one way, and if something else occurred, I'd respond in a different way). That's not how it was.

I don't know whether other activists are strategic, but I continued to trust my instincts as a mother. For me, one thing that did help was to take stock of what had happened in the previous year. That gave me a little clarity on what was successful, and what wasn't, and possibly helped lead me down the right path in the new year.

Putting so much of myself into that campaign was something I'd never change, because even though I did not see the outcome I had worked so hard for, I did reach many people. I met and talked with so many folks across the country, and I knew I had made a difference with lots of them. That was something to celebrate. I'd also met many powerful and influential people who listened and learned more about my mission. To me, all of that continued to lay the groundwork for the future. Each experience was another layer on the cake, and eventually that victory would be sweet.

Until then, I wasn't ready to give up. I could take all I had learned and try to use that to effect change, no matter how small. It felt like pieces of a huge jigsaw puzzle. Sometimes I could clearly see how certain experiences fit together. Other times I knew that there was a connection but wasn't exactly sure where it would fit to complete the picture. I realized that it was all right, though, because if it was meant to be, and if it was in God's plan, it would all become clear to me at the proper moment.

For me, working with Hillary's campaign did something that I had never expected. Prior to that, I had gathered with the other mothers on several occasions, most of them arranged by the National Action Network, Al Sharpton, or another civil liberties group. It was good for us because we came together with a similar message, and delivering it as a group got us more attention and helped to generate a conversation. The members were very fluid, and while some joined in more often than others, they all did what worked for them.

When Hillary and her campaign called us to that meeting in Chicago, there were about a dozen of us there. By getting us together and talking about what we could accomplish as a group, she helped to validate the mission we had started, and she helped us to see the power we shared collectively. Having a candidate for president come to us and ask for our help meant that we held even more potential than I ever realized. She was coming to us and asking us to come along on the ride with her. That meant that we were getting our message out there loudly enough for her to take notice.

Then, once on the campaign trail, I really got to know the other ladies much better. Before that, we had exchanged pleasantries and shared meals after some of the events, but we didn't know each other very well as people. We knew of the pain we had each endured, and the struggles, and challenges, because we talked about those right away. However, I never knew them as women. For me, that changed once we were traveling around the country. We spent a lot of time together and shared a lot of experiences, good and bad.

We didn't always get welcoming receptions. Some people were negative and didn't necessarily like the messages we delivered. That was fine with me because I didn't expect everyone to understand, but I didn't like the negative and hostile comments that were sometimes directed our way. For the most part, though, it was very positive, and it felt good to share all of that with the other ladies. I think we all knew that was a unique opportunity that had been placed in front of us. We were on the world stage, our words being transmitted all over. That was an amazing feeling.

To know that we were reaching people beyond the walls of a local event was a big responsibility and also a huge accomplishment for us. We had each been effective in our own way, but together, with this platform, it felt like we were really making a difference. Win or lose, our message would remain unchanged, as it always had. We wanted justice for our loved ones and protection for others. Losing an election wouldn't change that, and it wouldn't change us.

With each event and the more we shared of ourselves, the stronger our bond became. We learned about each other's families and hopes and dreams. It was interesting to hear how the other women had been handling the changes that come with these horrible incidents. I handled things the way that worked for me, and hearing the other stories gave me insight into how they approached things. We all had different outlooks and approaches. Other differentiators were our family situations and the tragedy itself.

With Eric, it was very public and very prolific. You couldn't help but hear about it. There was no avoiding it because of the video and because it happened in such a huge city like New York. That amplified everything and helped to keep it in the news because everything, even the local events, played out in the national news that comes out of the city. One of the first components of activism is visibility. That was not an issue for me because my cause was very clear each time that video was played. Some of the other situations were not as public or occurred in small towns where they didn't get the same amount of press coverage. So many of the women had to educate people first on what happened and why it was important. They did a great job of that—it was just one of the differences I noticed.

Another one was unfortunately when the incident happened. As with any criminal case, the older it gets, the less attention and focus tends to be on it, which is sad and can feel very defeating. I had concerns about that initially. Just because Eric's death was so public, the horrible reality was that there were more happening every day and each one demanded the attention of the public. At some point there is a level of saturation and sheer fatigue. People get tired of the sad, heartbreaking stories. I understood that reality because until it happened to me, I felt that way too. Each time I heard about another shooting or attack or death, I felt horrible for the victim and their family, but I didn't know what else to do, and I could only take so much before I wanted to tune it out.

I guess that's human nature, maybe a form of survival. We can only process so much bad news and negativity at a time. I was discovering that understanding some of the inner workings of human nature was very helpful because it clarified and validated a lot of my experiences. That didn't change the fact that one of our issues was keeping our cases out there in the news. Interest meant awareness and awareness meant a possibility of resolution. There were a lot of things to think about. It was a lot more than telling our story and then leaving. So much more.

As I learned more about the women, we formed a true connection and unity. The core group was me, Sybrina, Geneva, Lucy, Maria, and Cleo, but others came when possible. The more events we did, the more often we were recognized and the more welcoming our reception. It almost took on a life of its own by the sheer momentum that was propelled by the campaign. We were along for the ride, but we were there for the big picture. It was about much more than politics and winning an election. This was our lives and our families' lives that we were putting out there every day. We had to bare our souls each time with the hope that those listening would receive the message we were trying to convey. I also found it very helpful to observe the other ladies and how they handled everything. It was inevitable that we would compare notes and ask each other for critiques on how we were doing. When I first started out, I felt so uncomfortable and lost out there on a stage. I know that I wasn't polished and professional—probably the exact opposite!

That was all right, though, because it worked for me. People responded to my obvious reluctance to be in that situation. That was the truth. I was reluctant to be there because I didn't want to *have* to be there. I didn't want that to be my reality, but it was. So I had to make peace with that and then develop myself the best I could. Saying it was a learning experience and an evolution is an understatement. That's why I am so adamant about others getting out there and doing the same thing. I encourage others to get active because, like Cynthia Davis taught me, a lot of it is about just showing up.

I was proof that despite my hesitancy, I was making the most of it and doing things my way. That might not be what works for someone else, but that is just fine. It is about finding what is most comfortable for your personality and your experiences. For me, since Eric's death was so physical and violent and aggressive, I did not want to come across like that. First of all, that's not my personality, so it would go against my nature. Also, while that might be the way others choose to do things, I felt that took away from my message of fairness and education.

For me, it seemed like people were open to receiving the message I was trying to convey if I did it my way, coming across direct but soft spoken and sure of myself. People would tell me that I came across as a concerned mother, and they related to that. So that was my way of sharing the message of police reform and brutality. By example, I was showing that the issue could be addressed in a calm, mature manner. Truthfully, sometimes inside I just wanted to scream at them: "How could you allow this to happen to my son? How is this acceptable behavior? How do you sleep at night?"

I guess we all have moments like that when we are doing things one way, but on the inside—oh, if we could just let it all out, it would feel so good. However, I couldn't allow myself that brief moment of satisfaction because it could undermine all of my work. There were already some folks in the Black Lives Matter movement taking a more aggressive approach. I let them do it their way, and I did it mine. Hopefully our combined efforts and different methods of delivery would get results. Plus, if there were times when I did feel the need to vent, Ben and the rest of my family were always there to listen.

Touring as a group helped bring us mothers together in more of a cohesive unit. We remained pliable, with some joining and some sitting events out, but it was like we had a rhythm going where when one of us was absent, someone else could fill in and make sure our message was covered. Just because it wasn't one woman's own experience didn't mean that she couldn't bring up the topic, often mentioning the other mother as an example people could relate to. As we got to know each other better, we were able to fill in for each other and help the audience connect the dots. We developed our own unspoken cues where we knew when to jump in or add to the conversation. We all tried to give each other plenty of time to talk and share, but we also made sure to back each other up and show support.

It was important for us to come across exactly as we were, mothers from different backgrounds and situations with our only initial similarities being the death of our children and the fact that we were Black. As we got to know each other, we learned about each of our unique strengths and challenges. So when we needed to lean on each other, we could do that, knowing we all had that sisterhood and connection.

Like any group of people who come together based purely on circumstance, we were not all instant, lifelong friends. That was the truth. We discovered that we are all strong, confident women in our own right and with our own opinions. Those who chose to travel and campaign with Hillary agreed with her message and supported her, so we had that in common. That was another thing that united us. Some did not join her simply because that was not right for them. Hillary certainly understood that and made it very clear on that day in Chicago that if we were not 100 percent behind her and her mission, the campaign trail was not for us. Only those who truly wanted to be there should go. The others could pursue whatever worked for them. There was no pressure for all of us to be the same and believe the same things.

There were members of my family who supported Bernie Sanders, Hillary's Democratic opponent, so I understood that not everyone was going to feel the same way. I handled that like everything else: I let them be and understood that they had a right to their beliefs and I had a right to mine. To me, that's part of being a family, understanding that just because we are all related doesn't mean we think the same and agree on everything. What it does mean is that we put aside those differences when the time comes and focus on being together.

As far as the Mothers of the Movement are concerned, I don't know whether it was Hillary's plan all along, but bringing us on the road with her really helped our group come together in many ways. Previously, if there was an event in another city and a mother couldn't get there, she didn't attend. It was more a matter of logistics and finances. On the campaign trail, Hillary's team made sure that we got to every event we wanted to go to. That removed the issues of geography and finances. As I had learned as an activist, the best way to get people to show up is to make it as convenient as possible. That's what Hillary's camp did by making sure that we were all in the same place at the same time.

Making that possible gave our group more structure than it had before, and I realized that as each month passed we were becoming more comfortable with each other and stronger and more effective as a group. That cohesion and those experiences helped us form a stronger and more productive bond. I don't know whether that was Hillary's intent, but maybe it was because she's a smart woman.

We left the campaign trail and the election, not victorious, but with a definite feeling that we were a strong force, especially collectively. The power of a group of mothers was undeniable. I felt energized and comforted that even though our candidate hadn't won the presidency, many positive things came out of the campaign, one of them being a stronger Mothers of the Movement group.

I wasn't sure where we would take the group in the future because we no longer had the campaign trail to hold us together. I just hoped the bonds we had formed would continue and that we would unite when it made sense. The group is unique in that it isn't formal or structured. It's almost like when a group of mothers comes together to help each other with babysitting and running errands. We were essentially doing the same thing with the movement. We were pooling our collective experiences and using them so that we could all benefit. Of course, the only benefit we all wanted was to see justice served for our children and to see real change, particularly when it came to the way Blacks were treated by anyone in a law enforcement capacity.

With the new year, I had hopes the Mothers would come together when we could, but I also knew I had to continue along my own path. I still had work to do, and the new administration meant new challenges. I had learned so much from being so involved in politics, and I decided that I would find as many opportunities as I could to get involved and make sure the new administration did not take us back to the dark, scary times before the Civil Rights Act. That might sound kind of dramatic and alarmist, but with all the hate speech flying around, I was not taking anything for granted.

This was the first time I was being proactive in what I called my unplanned activism. I wanted to build on that last year's efforts and the huge exposure that we had. I needed to find ways to keep my face out in the public eye so that I could keep Eric's name in people's mouths. I wanted them saying "Eric Garner" because that kept him in the consciousness. I wanted him to be as real and present for them as he was for me every day. I never let his memory fade, and I hoped that I could make sure others didn't forget, either. My mission was awareness, and it started on January 14, 2017.

That day, I joined Al Sharpton, the National Action Network, and many others for a rally at West Potomac Park in Washington, DC. We were there to celebrate and honor the eighty-eighth anniversary of the birth of Dr. Martin Luther King Jr. All across the country there were observances and community service events. In DC, there was a parade and peace walk that is a tradition, and there were also tributes, speeches, and church services.

When you are involved in raising public awareness, the weather is not always your friend, and you cannot always count on a beautiful day for an event. In fact, it's usually the opposite. I don't know whether it's Murphy's law or what, but a lot of activists I know have talked about times when they planned a beautiful event down to the last detail only to be faced with challenging weather.

That day in Washington was cold and rainy, but as I stood in front of the monument of the inspirational Dr. King, I didn't care about a little rain. It was very easy to allow roadblocks to slow me down, but I wasn't about to give in to that. Reverend Al Sharpton spoke at the event and did not disappoint. I am learning in this journey to celebrate the strengths of others and allow those to shine, just as they did for me. They allowed me to do things in the manner that worked for me, and I did the same for them. I will never be the passionate speaker that Reverend Sharpton is, but I will continue on my own journey in my own way.

His speech was called "We Shall Not Be Moved," and a rally followed. Reverend Sharpton and the National Action Network team are very good about getting everyone fired up, and that day was no exception. I heard chants like "We will not be moved" and "No justice, no peace."

This rally was a bit different because hiding just below the surface of our enthusiasm and reverence for Dr. King was the horrible reality of the incoming team. Many of the speakers, including Congressman John Lewis, spoke about not attending the next week's inauguration, and they encouraged the Democratic representatives to stand up to the incoming administration's policies of divisiveness. There was also talk about working to oppose the incoming attorney general, the one who would replace Loretta Lynch. It was Senator Jeff Sessions, whom I hadn't heard a lot about before, but what I learned that day had me worried that Eric's case would never get a fair shot with him in office.

It was good to reconnect with Sybrina Fulton after the crazy campaign ride we had been on the previous year. Each time we got together, we compared notes and talked about things we were working on, our successes and challenges, and the hopes we clung to. Though I share a special bond with each of them, I am not best friends with any of the mothers. We all lead our own lives and do things the way we see fit. I respect what they do, and it feels good to reconnect with them because they are the only ones who truly know what it's like.

My other family members understand, don't get me wrong about that. However, our shared connection as mothers whose children were murdered is something that is so unique it really helps to speak to another person like Sybrina. Also, her tragedy occurred in 2012, so she has been working for reform a little longer than I have and she's always ready to share anything she has learned. As mothers, that's what we all try to do.

I found myself back in Washington a week later for the Women's March on Washington. The Martin Luther King event had a great turnout, but this event was the hugest gathering that I'd ever seen. I found out after that it was the largest single-day demonstration in U.S. history. It was said that there were marches not only in Washington, DC, but also in more than 650 other cities across the country. Supposedly there were also marches in hundreds of other countries. In Washington, DC, alone, more than five hundred thousand women and their supporters were estimated to have taken to the streets.

Naturally there were many politicians and celebrities, but the people who impressed me the most were the everyday women and others who took time to attend. They left their families and traveled by plane, car, train, and bus to get to the march and let the new president know that they were not going to be silent. I thought it was kind of funny that he complained about his small inauguration, because if he wanted a lot of people in the streets of Washington, he sure got them that day.

Some people felt a certain way because they didn't see this kind of turnout at their events. There were complaints that some of the more focused Black Lives Matter events got much less attendance and usually less press. I didn't focus on that too much because I know that you cannot taunt or guilt people into attending anything. It has to be something they want to do from their heart. The focus needs to be on creating within them a desire to get involved. I understand that is not easy to do, but it's really the only way.

I saw this as a positive step toward folks getting on their feet in the name of activism. I'd learned from the National Action Network team that if people show up and have a positive experience, it helps to show them that they can do it and that they can make a difference. So that's what I hoped for with that event. It was also encouraging because it was organized by and for women. That gave me some real hope because that's what we had been doing for the last year, touring and campaigning as mothers and women. Several of the Mothers of the Movement attended to show our support, including Sybrina, Lucy McBath, Maria Hamilton, and me.

I'm not saying we were groundbreakers or anything like that, but it did feel good and validating to see that other women were showing up and getting active just as we had been doing for Hillary. I would like to say that maybe we played a small part in that, but I'm sure it was primarily because of Hillary and the fact that the reality of the first female president was not to be in 2017. Regardless of the motivation, it was very exciting to witness and be a part of history.

It made me think back to when I had just started. I had no idea what I was doing. I was just propelled by my grief. Ben and I were stricken and trying to come to terms with our son's death. I channeled my energy into activism. Ben did things a little differently. He joined me on the marches and any of the big events where I needed him, but he also put his handyman skills to good use. I met him way back when I was living in government housing and he was a window installer, so he had always been good at construction and repairs.

At first, people created an informal shrine at the site of Eric's murder, leaving flowers and candles and signs and posters on the sidewalk beside the Bay Beauty Supply store. Graffiti artists painted signs nearby referencing "I can't breathe" and other tributes to his memory. So Ben built a makeshift memorial to place on the sidewalk. It's made of thick plastic on all sides so people can see inside, and it has a hinged lid with a lock on it. Ben visits the site and puts any flowers, candles, and other things that people leave inside the box. That way they are out of the elements but also on display for anyone who wants to visit. There's a wreath above it and a poster that includes the words "No indictment, no conviction, no justice."

Someone destroyed it about a week after he built it, but Ben cleaned up the mess and built another one. He said he will keep building them as long as necessary because Eric deserves that. I'm sure it's not legal to have it on the sidewalk, but no one has defaced it since then. So I guess maybe us older folks are a little more active and involved than we realized we were.

When I left that women's march, I took away from it the images of all the powerful, determined women I had seen, and the dedication in their faces just helped to fuel my mission even more. Having witnessed people of all ages and races brave the cold and discomfort, it helped me realize that women really can make a difference, something I would have never thought possible even just a few years ago. It felt good not only to witness change but also, in my own way, to be a part of it.

The main thing that I took away, and that I think a lot of others did as well, was the positivity and sense of hopefulness that it helped to instill in me. An important aspect of activism is making sure people can sustain their drive and enthusiasm. It's one of those things that, no matter how committed someone appears to be, if they don't feel it, they can't effectively convey it to others. If you're in it for the wrong reasons, hoping to meet important people or hang with celebrities or further your career, people can sense that.

I've watched people come and go, and the ones who last are those who truly have it inside them. It's something that's not easy to explain or describe, but I know it when I see it. Time flies, but at this point I guess I've been doing this for more than four years, so I've picked up on things along the way. I've seen very sincere folks join the cause only to realize that it isn't right for them. They may not have intentionally gotten involved in something they didn't wholeheartedly believe in, but along the way it becomes obvious when someone's heart is just not in it and that's really where it counts. It has to be part of your heart and soul and spirit. If you're in it for other reasons, it's great that you showed up, but it's just not going to work.

For some people who want to be involved in a movement, it's about finding the right fit. Just because you see someone out there making a statement and you support them or find their cause to be a noble one, that doesn't necessarily mean it's for you. Often there is a trial-and-error aspect where folks need to get in there and try it on for size. If it doesn't work for you, believe me, there are many other important causes that can use help.

Another important thing to remember is that protests and speeches and marches are not the only ways to get involved. There are so many other aspects that I sure didn't know about at first, either. When I got involved with the National Action Network, and for me doing that was not something I was sure about at the time, I learned so much about what it takes to get things done. There's being on the front lines the way me and the other mothers are, but there are other areas that are just as important, if not more so. Things like lobbying politicians and helping with research also help to support change.

I'm not an expert on all of that. I can only speak on what has worked for me and advise others to get in touch with an organization like NAN or something similar. The unfortunate reality is that there are so many organizations because there are so many causes and there is so much need. While that can be overwhelming to think about, I choose to look on the positive side. That means there are many ways that people can get involved in something that is special to them and close to their heart.

After I got back to New York, I had already been in two large demonstrations in Washington, DC, and the year had just started. I huddled up with Nadia and shared with her that I was still not satisfied. I wanted to do more. Seeing those folks come out in the cold gave me the strength to keep pushing on. Without Hillary's campaign to fill my calendar, I could find other things that worked for me, and Nadia could help. She was very motivated as well, and she also realized that without a presidential campaign, I had to shift my focus, and if I didn't handle it right, it could sideline my momentum.

That's one of the things I haven't talked about—having some great people to help you is always a good thing. That's not really necessary at the beginning, and if I'd had that early on, I'm not sure it would have been beneficial because I was still processing things. I wasn't in the frame of mind where I could think about the future. As far as I was concerned, my future was killed that day on Bay Street.

Time has an amazing way of allowing us to deal with our memories and keep moving on. I'm not exactly sure when I reached that point, but it was very gradual. My one-step-at-a-time method allowed me to process my feelings while still doing some work on Eric's behalf. At first I think I was still a bit dazed, but slowly, gradually, that pain and hopelessness morphed and changed inside me. It was almost like giving birth again. The idea of activism took hold slowly. I kept feeding it with each new event I attended or march I walked in or speech I gave.

I don't think it was until the Dr. King March and the Women's March following right after that I realized there were many opportunities beyond the political realm. There were many other ways I could stay involved and stay visible. I would keep Eric's name and image in the public eye for as long as I was able, and Nadia would help me do that with her ideas and her contacts. However, I don't think anyone expected what was to come next. I know I sure didn't.

It was the last day of a very busy month, January 31, 2017. I was back in New York, and I joined my friends from NAN, including minister Kirsten John Foy and Al Sharpton's daughter Ashley, who was director of a youth group. We were at Trump Tower in

Manhattan protesting the recent Supreme Court nomination of a man named Judge Neil Gorsuch to fill the vacancy left when Antonin Scalia died last year (and the Republicans had refused to allow the Obama nominee to fill the seat, instead delaying the nomination until they were in power and could make their own choice). Folks were also marching in Brooklyn and other sections of New York, and in other cities, to protest the nomination.

This was a much more targeted protest than I had been involved with in the past. Previously I was more involved with marches and town halls and speaking on panels. Protesting political decisions was new for me, but I was willing to try it and see what happened. I had the support of the Network, and I knew that having recognizable faces would help generate attention, and it sure did.

I ended up being led away from there with my hands behind my back in plastic restraints as the police took me down the street, one on each arm. Others were arrested as well, and we were taken to the police station and charged with civil disobedience. At least I think that was the official charge. It was strange to be led down the street in restraints, but I wasn't scared or intimidated. I knew it was important to raise awareness, and I also understood the risks. Being recognizable, I realized that if anyone were arrested, it would be me, and I was right about that.

NAN sent out a statement that read, "In an act of civil disobedience and in the tradition of Dr. Martin Luther King Jr., Eric Garner's mom and others were arrested tonight in front of Trump Tower over President Trump's Supreme Court nominee Neil Gorsuch."

Some of my family members were especially concerned, but I told them not to worry about me. Ellisha couldn't believe her mother, the grandmother of her children, was on the news with cuffs on. I realized that they would want to make a display of it and take my picture, which they did. It was on the front page of a lot of papers and websites. It's still feels a little surreal that I can type "Gwen Carr arrested" in a web browser and my image pops up.

I guess that's what we get for blocking traffic on Fifth Avenue. Oh, I left that part out, didn't I? Sometimes to get attention and a reaction, we have to cause a little disruption, so we were out there messing up that crazy Manhattan traffic. That's a tip that I can share with you: Messing up how folks get around always gets a lot of attention. People don't like when their routine is impacted, and it always gets a reaction.

Nadia wasn't too happy that I had gotten arrested. She knew what I was going to do, and she advised me to be careful, but she was shocked that it turned out like it had. I suppose no publicist likes to wake up to a news alert about their client being arrested. She made her peace with it, though, because she had another idea. She proposed that I write a book about my experiences. That way I could share my story and how I handled Eric's murder. It was her thought that other people would get a better sense of what I had been going through and what I'd dealt with over the past few years.

I agreed that it would be great, but just like I was no activist, I was definitely not a writer. Nadia assured me that she would figure it out, and she did. She found a literary agent and a cowriter who promised to help me through the entire process. That was exactly what I needed because I had big plans for the year and I knew that writing a book was a big undertaking. The agent and writer were both located in the Washington, DC, area, so Nadia had another idea. She proposed that we go meet them, establish a relationship, and maybe get some preliminary interviews done as well.

She also suggested that we pay a little visit to the White House. Prior to the new administration coming in, Eric's case had supposedly been moved from the civil to the criminal division of the Department of Justice. Civil cases would focus on whether a person's civil rights were violated. A criminal case would suggest that criminal charges may be filed. We didn't have anything definite because everything is confidential, but if it had moved, that meant that maybe there would be some decision to proceed with charges.

In March, we made our way to the nation's capital for a full day of meetings. First, we met with Dave, the cowriter, at our hotel lounge. He asked me questions and recorded me as I told my story as best I could. I tried to get in all the details I could think of, and Nadia was there to confirm some of the timeline. I never thought it was so detailed and involved. I had been living it, but to retell it to someone and put it all into some type of order that makes sense was a new world for me. Once again, I was learning something new, and I was grateful for that.

After the interviews, we had a quick lunch and said our good-byes to Dave so we could head to our next appointment. We made our way downtown and arrived at the White House. Nadia had already called our contact, Omarosa Manigault-Newman. At the time I believe her title was director of communications of public liaison. Nadia had been in touch with her, and she agreed to talk with us. I wasn't sure what to expect because there had been a lot of stories about her, especially because of her role as a "villain" on some reality shows, including *The Apprentice*.

For some reason we had an issue getting inside the White House. I guess security had been tightened and we were supposedly on a list, but not on *the* list. I don't know what was going on, but Nadia explained it to Omarosa, and she said, "No problem. I'll come down and we can go to the café on the corner to talk." So that's what we did.

I was pleasantly surprised because she talked to us on a personal level, not as an official or a politician. She was very nice to us. I told her that I don't agree with the party she was aligned with, but I thought that she was a kind and compassionate person and I hoped that she could help us get some information about Eric's case. We talked with her for more than two hours. I stressed that the U.S. Department of Justice was really our last resort and trying to get answers from anyone over there was almost impossible. We had even gone there before but couldn't find out anything.

It was my hope that maybe she could call over there and at least see whether they would give her some information on what was planned. I know it wasn't going to be an official announcement or anything like that, but I just thought on a personal level she could at least try to get something from them. At that point, legally, that was really our last option. There had been talk about the FBI going back and forth between New York agents and federal agents and the need for an independent prosecutor.

I wondered that if that issue kept coming up, why wasn't anything being done to address it? To me, it seemed like there should be an automatic trigger that an impartial prosecutor unaffiliated with the departments involved in a case was required. It didn't make sense to me that it would even be a question. While these men were arguing about whose territory it was and which jurisdiction and this and that, lives were at stake. It was ridiculous.

We realized that we were late for our dinner with Diane, my literary agent, and Dave had also agreed to join us at a place in the Adams Morgan section of Washington. We finally got there, a little late, but we made it. When we arrived, we saw that April Ryan, the White House correspondent I'd met before, was there with them. I knew she was with the same high-powered agent, which was fine, but I was a little surprised that she was at our dinner.

Regardless, we all sat down and started to talk. Things went very well, and we were having a good time. Then April asked where we had been, and I told her that we had met with Omarosa at the White House, hoping to find out something about Eric's case at the DOJ. She asked me whether she could interview me about it. To be honest, I was caught off guard because I hadn't planned anything, and it had just happened. I also knew that we hadn't gone through proper channels and just hoped to get any morsel of information.

April pulled out a recorder at the dinner table and asked me where we were earlier and what we hoped to accomplish by talking to Omarosa. I answered as best I could and hoped I didn't say anything that would hinder whatever progress Omarosa was able to make. I told April that I wanted them to take an objective look at my son's case and maybe we would get some kind of a positive outcome. I wanted to see the police officers held accountable for their misconduct. Nadia gave me the side eye the entire time. Once we were done, April thanked me and left. We talked more about the book and our ideas for it and finished eating.

The next day there were headlines everywhere, like the one in the *Daily News* that read "Eric Garner's mother meets with Trump aide Omarosa Manigault to get update on federal probe of son's death." The White House press secretary, Sean Spicer, was in the news saying that it was inappropriate for us to meet. I thought, *Now I've really messed up*. My phone rang all that day, everyone looking for a comment. I didn't know what to do.

Nadia told me that I hadn't really messed up, but I needed to understand the difference between talking to the media to get Eric's name out and giving information that could jeopardize the investigation. I know April was just doing her job, and I also know she and Omarosa did not get along, but I wasn't thinking about all of that at the time. I was just thinking about Eric. One reporter did get hold of me, and he tried to get me to give him a comment.

"Do you have any comment on your White House visit?" he asked.

I responded, "Oh, you mean when I met Barack Obama?" I knew that wasn't what he meant, but I decided to play into the naïve grandmother stereotype some people have of me. Maybe I would get the hang of the crazy public relations world after all.

July 2017 marked the third anniversary of the death of my first-born child. This event wasn't as lavish as the previous one, and there was no surprise visit from Beyoncé, but it was a time for us to honor Eric. I was pleasantly surprised when many of the mothers were able to show up. It was a huge list including Margarita Rosario (Anthony Rosario), Carol Gray (Kimani Gray), Constance Malcolm (Ramarley Graham), Hawa Bah (Mohamed Bah), Iris Baez (Anthony Baez), Valerie Bell (Sean Bell), Nicholas Heyward (Nicholas Heyward Jr.), Victor Dempsey (Delrawn Small), Auntie (Akai Gurley), Natasha Duncan (Shantel Davis), Kadi Diallo (Amadou Diallo), Wanda Johnson (Oscar Grant), Lezley McSpadden (Michael Brown), Samaria Rice (Tamir Rice), Queen Brown (Eviton Brown), Marion Gray-Hopkins (Gary Hopkins Jr.), Greta Willis (Kevin L. Cooper), Rhanda Dormeus (Korryn Gaines), Gwendolyn Wesley (Clifford Wesley), Cynthia D. Dawkins (Timothy Dawkins), Beverly Smith (Alonzo Smith), Pam Brooks (Amir Brooks), Gina Best (India Kager), Nardyne Jefferies (Brishell Jones), Bridzette Lane (Raphael Briscoe), Burnett McFadden (Randolph, Reginald, Linton McFadden), and Sheila Banks (Corey Jones).

There may have been more. I think it was the most mothers gathered at one of Eric's events, and I was eternally grateful. El-lisha helped with some of the organization, and I had Ben back on the grill. We went to my two supportive churches, Christian Love and New Hope, and then after the services we visited Eric's grave site before returning to the church for dinner. It wasn't fancy or stuffy—just a nice gathering of people who wanted to commemo-rate Eric and come together for some fellowship. We all wore white on Sunday to show our unity.

In September, we got some positive news, but then found out that it wasn't quite what it had initially appeared to be. New York City has a Civilian Complaint Review Board (CCRB), which is an independent agency that investigates complaints against New York City police officers. It's composed of city residents who investigate impartially and then send their findings to the police commissioner. The CCRB issued a recommendation that officer Daniel Pantaleo receive the strictest and most severe charges from the New York Police Department. Unfortunately, much like the coroner's report, nothing was done. We found out that recommendations like that are just basically suggestions and the NYPD and the mayor have the option of whether to take action. Their alternative is to wait for the federal investigation, so of course that was the path they chose—to do nothing.

Any time incidents like that come up, it reminds me why I do this "unplanned activism" of mine. It is so automatic for us to take the easy way and either not get involved or pass the buck. At first it shocked me when folks in authority positions would tell me to my face that there was nothing they could do when I knew that was not true. Still I smiled and went along with it. Like the way I dealt with that reporter on the phone, I tried to use people's perceptions of me to my advantage. As an activist, you learn that each situation is different, and challenges will present themselves with little notice. There's no one way to handle them, but, as I learned with that im-promptu interview, if you're not careful, you can get T-boned.

Nadia came to me with yet another opportunity, this one a tele-vision show. A production company was working with actress Viola

Davis and her husband to create a four-part series spotlighting the deaths of Black people at the hands of the police. The format was that they would talk to the family of the deceased to get their side and then meet with law enforcement representatives to hear things from their perspective. The title of the docu-series was appropriately *Two Sides* and would air on the Black-owned TV One.

Four episodes were planned, so Nadia worked with them to make sure Eric's story was the first one to air. She knew that there would be a lot of initial publicity and having such a high-profile story would be the best way to start the series. They promised to use Eric's case as the first episode. They sent out the following press release:

> *Two Sides* is a landmark limited four-part docu-series exploring watershed moments for law enforcement and the Black community at the crossroads between life and death, premiering Monday, January 22 at 10 p.m. ET on TV One. Executive produced by Academy Award winner Viola Davis, Julius Tennon (JuVee Productions) and Lemuel Plummer (L. Plummer Media) with narration by Davis, each one-hour episode of *Two Sides* offers an in-depth, comprehensive look into disturbing cases of officer-involved deaths.
>
> Focusing on four headline-grabbing fatal police encounters during 2014–2015, the series analyzes and presents multiple points of view of the highly charged cases involving Eric Garner (New York), Ezell Ford (California), John Crawford (Ohio), and Sandra Bland (Texas). Their tragic deaths sparked grassroots social justice movements such as Black Lives Matter, inspired protests by high-profile personalities, and immortalized their names as tragic figures in the polarizing debate on police brutality and race.
>
> "*Two Sides* continues TV One's mission to represent the issues and concerns of the importance to the Black community," says D'Angela Proctor, TV One Head of Original Programming and Production. "Inspired by courageous acts such as NBA Champions LeBron James and the Cleveland Cavaliers who donned 'I Can't Breathe' shirts in honor of Garner during pregame warm-ups, and the NFL's Colin Kaepernick who kneeled during the anthem prior to games for an entire season to raise awareness

of police brutality, we wanted to utilize our platform to shine a light on this pressing issue. We're honored to work with Viola and Julius, who have been active voices in the fight for equality to explore both sides of this dynamic equation, which continues to dominate social and political discourse in America."

JuVee executive producers Davis and Tennon both hope the show can help expand the dialogue around these incidents and provide an opportunity for real change to occur.

"With *Two Sides* you'll hear how the incident transpired and how it affected change or did not affect change. And, how the families are still being affected," said Davis and Tennon in a joint statement. "This is a way for us to humanize these victims and not make them just a statistic. We also have to look at the other side of the story—our law enforcement's point of view. Let's come together and have a conversation around these issues so that we can come up with real solutions that will lead to positive change."

In addition to discussing the circumstances leading to the victims' fateful encounter with police, in each episode of *Two Sides* family and friends share their heartbreaking accounts of where they were when their loved ones died, along with fond memories and recollections of their young lives. Law enforcement experts and independent commentators offer expertise and opinions on each incident with explanations of police regulations and procedures, as well as an analysis of the many factors involved in each of these four unique events.

The series also features commentary from high-profile contributors such as activist Rev. Al Sharpton, Congresswoman Maxine Waters and attorney Christopher Darden, as well as representatives from various law enforcement agencies and other notable pundits.

"There are two sides to every story," says Rev. Al Sharpton in the premiere episode. "I believe the policeman has a side; I believe the victim has a side; But there is only one truth."

"These cases sparked controversy that ignited a necessary movement throughout our country," says TV One General Manager Michelle Rice. "The relationship between law enforcement and the African American community has been a precarious one for far too long and the conversation around reform must continue. There is a historical and deep divide that needs to be mended. We are privileged to present this unique series which offers an in-depth look into each story from two different perspectives, and hopefully influences an honest dialogue on the fractured state of police-community relations."

**FEATURED CASES:**

- ERIC GARNER (43)—STATEN ISLAND, NY
  In the summer of 2014, Eric Garner was choked and killed by NYPD officers while being arrested. The 43-year-old was standing outside of a beauty supply store in Staten Island, New York, when police tried to arrest him for allegedly illegally selling loose cigarettes. The video of Officer Daniel Pantaleo putting Garner in a chokehold went viral. Although the medical examiner ruled his death a homicide, a grand jury has thus far declined to indict Pantaleo.

- EZELL FORD (25)—LOS ANGELES, CA
  Ezell Ford died at 25-years-old in August 2014 after being shot three times in the back during a scuffle with Los Angeles Police Department Officers Sharlton Wampler and Antonio Villegas. Competing accounts of the events surrounding Ford's death sparked unrest and demonstrations. Almost two years later, in June 2016, the Los Angeles Board of Police Commissioners concluded that only one of the officers was justified in the shooting. Upon receiving the ruling, the Ford family filed a lawsuit against the LAPD claiming $75 million in damages; the case was eventually settled out of court.

- JOHN CRAWFORD (22)—DAYTON, OH
  John Crawford III was shot by officers while carrying a BB gun at a Wal-Mart store in Beavercreek, Ohio. Crawford was only 22-years-old at the time of his death in August 2014. A grand jury failed to indict Officer Sean Williams and Sgt. David Darkow, leading to protests by members of the Black Lives Matter movement.

- SANDRA BLAND (28)—HEMPSTEAD, TX
  In the summer of 2015, Sandra Bland was found hanging in her jail cell after being arrested at a traffic stop three days prior.

Her death was ultimately ruled a suicide but Bland's family disagrees. The dispute over Bland's cause of death led to unrest in communities across the nation.

*Two Sides* is produced for TV One by L. Plummer Media in partnership with JuVee Productions. Lemuel Plummer and Jason Tolbert of L. Plummer Media and Viola Davis, Julius Tennon and Andrew T. Wang of JuVee Productions serve as Executive Producers. For TV One, D'Angela Proctor is SVP, Original Programming & Production and shares executive in charge of production duties with Robyn Greene Arrington, VP, Original Programming & Production.

That October, the production company visited us and set up interviews with various family members. We spent several days talking with production, filming interviews, and visiting various locations in the city. I wasn't sure what they were going to use once they put it all together, but I did hope that having an entire episode focused on Eric's case was a big deal and would garner a lot of publicity. It was part of the new strategy Nadia and I were implementing to use my time as effectively as I could. I was impressed with how they seemed to take care to really listen to what we had to say and why we felt so discouraged by state and federal authorities.

I wanted to stress that I did not want to be portrayed any differently than how I truly felt. I didn't want to come off as out of touch or particularly vindictive. I know how TV shows can film interviews and then change things around when they are edited so they come out differently than it was described. It made me think of Omarosa and how she came across on some of the shows she was on. I don't know who the true person is, but she seemed so different in person from what I'd seen on TV.

So that was one of my concerns. Would we be portrayed accurately and respectfully? They assured me that I did not need to be concerned, and the fact that Viola Davis was connected to the project did help me feel better because she seems to be involved in quality productions. Putting trust in people you don't know is scary, especially when they are telling the story of how your son was

killed. It's important that it be explained accurately, especially because of the circumstances and because it is reportedly still under
investigation.

I can't imagine what I would do if I participated in a project and
was then disappointed with the final product. They had my son's
memory in their hands and they would be reaching a wide audience, so I had cause to be concerned. When I was sharing my story
of Eric, I could control what I said and how I responded to questions. After filming scenes and sitting for interviews, I had to put
my trust in them to come up with something that paid tribute to my
son. I did not approach the project without carefully weighing the
pros and cons. Naturally, Nadia stayed involved with the production
company and continued to relay my concerns prior to its airing on
national television.

By January 2018, the first episode was ready, and, just as Nadia
had predicted, there was a lot of publicity. It was hyped everywhere,
and with Viola Davis involved it continued to generate interest.
Nadia accompanied me to the premiere in Los Angeles as part of
the NAACP Image Awards. TV host Roland Martin was the mod-
erator, and I spoke on a panel about the episode along with the
production company. As often happened, I was the family member
there to represent Eric even though other relatives appeared on
the episode, even Ben and Ellisha. Al Sharpton was also included,
which I appreciated since he had been there from day one.

It was interesting watching that premiere and seeing how we
were portrayed. As promised, they took care to show us with as few
edits as possible, so I was happy with how we came across, and I was
proud of how everyone conducted themselves since I hadn't seen
their interviews before then. I understood why they included interviews with experts that represented the point of view of the police
department, even though I didn't particularly like what they said. I
argued with everything they said under my breath, but I stayed calm
and composed. Just because there were two sides didn't mean that
they were both the right side.

After I returned home, the show aired on TV One the next week,
and we all gathered around to watch it. When it was over, I received

so many calls from people eager to share their opinion of the program with me. Not everyone loved it, but they all thought it was well done and balanced. It was a huge relief because I was so nervous about how it would turn out. That week it debuted, I accompanied Julius Tennon and some people from the production company and TV One to do some national publicity for the show. We were on the *Megyn Kelly Show* first, then countless other TV shows followed by a slew of radio interviews. It was a busy week. Fortunately, it was all in New York, so I didn't have to go too far. Once again, I found myself as the default representative for the family, a role I was becoming accustomed to, just like my unplanned activism.

Next, I filmed a segment on an episode of the series *The Quad*, which airs on BET and focuses on campus life at a fictional HBCU named Georgia A&M University, with a group of diverse students. The episode I am in deals with police brutality and is very powerful. There's even a rap song that accompanies the episode, and I narrate some of the lyrics and the beginning and the end of the song. That was another of Nadia's "gets" for me as she continues helping me connect with people and, most important, keep Eric Garner's name out there.

Sometimes I stop and think about everything that has happened after July 17, 2014, that fateful day when my son was taken from me. I would never have imagined that I'd be doing some of the things that I've done or gone to the places I've visited or met the incredible people who have crossed paths with me. There has been so much support and guidance and love along the way that it opened me up to a whole new life at a time when I had expected to retire and take it easy. Before all of this happened, I thought that maybe I would do some traveling. I'd often tease that I was going to move away to a life of leisure, but I know that I'll never leave smoggy old New York.

These days I'm much more protective of my daughter Ellisha, even though she has her own life and doesn't need me interfering, but that's a mother's job. All the time, I tell her to be careful because she is all I have left. I stress that a lot of people just say, "Be careful," but that I really mean that she needs to pay attention and use good judgment at all times. If I hear about a bus crash or some other emergency in the city, I call immediately to check on her. I need her to stay around. I don't need anything to happen to my baby girl.

She will call often just to check on me and see how I'm doing. She will tell me a silly joke or something funny that one of the kids has done. She says that her two boys are like the way Eric and Emery used to be. It's like they are back in a different form. I don't mean to do it, but sometimes I do call Mikey "Eric" and I'll refer to Junior as "Emery," and they will answer me! I'm sure they think Grandma is just being silly, but it makes me feel good when they respond to those names.

It hasn't all been lights and cameras. There was a situation when I was attending a commemoration in Oakland, California. I was in the airport and received an anonymous phone call saying that my daughter had been kidnapped and the caller wanted me to give them money. That was scary because I couldn't get hold of Ellisha and had to get the authorities involved so they could locate her. Someone finally found her, and a nice police officer at the airport helped to facilitate everything and then calm me down. I appreciated him like I appreciate all responsible, caring law enforcement officers.

Situations like that come about because, for some reason, people have the misguided notion that I received money from a settlement. I guess it's a common thought that if a relative is involved in a situation like mine, we all get some type of payout. I can promise you that is not the case. Sometimes there are settlements and sometimes not. In Eric's case there was a settlement awarded, but not to me. It went to his wife and children. I was not part of that, and many of the other mothers have similar stories. If your child is killed and he's an adult with his own family, those are his immediate relatives, and they are the recipients. I suppose it shouldn't come as a surprise that, as mothers, we are last in line. It's another sacrifice we gladly make. Don't get me wrong, I have nothing against having money, but it's not my goal in life. After all that has happened to me, I've learned to take things as they come and be grateful and thankful for each day. Life and family are too precious to take for granted.

Cynthia Davis still marvels about how far I've come since we started out on those lonely days standing out in front of the Staten Island post office. She pushed me and said that she knew I could do it. She has even asked me to run for office, but I'm not ready for something like that. I was thrust into this activist life, and I'm not in it to win it. I'm fighting for those who can't. She calls me a champion and a soldier.

Nadia told me that she's seen my speaking style change. In the beginning, sometimes I would be worried about what to say or how to say it, but with her encouragement I've come a long way. Tragedy has fueled me and pushed me beyond my limits. Recently I had a huge speaking event at Nassau Community College. I thought that I was speaking to a classroom or a small department, and it turned out to be in front of thousands. I couldn't believe what I had to do. Nadia helped me get my talking points together, but I didn't rehearse or write anything down. I just gave them me, and that seemed to be exactly what they wanted.

Ben says that I've turned Eric's death into strength and started fighting for him and for everybody who no longer has a voice. He promised that he would stand by me on my new journey even though neither of us had any idea what to expect, and we still don't. Things change every day. New opportunities come up and there are also many disappointments as well, but I'm handling those much better these days. Somehow, by going through all of this, I've learned how to handle sadness and disappointment without letting it overtake me. Maybe that's one of the lessons I'm supposed to take away from this life. This has taught me how to be a better version of myself.

Now I've come to terms with the fact that this is what I do. Maybe this was my calling, and I just never knew it. As the mother of two deceased sons, I've had to get used to a lot of things, but one of the most difficult was the way people refer to me in person and in print. In person, I'm always "Eric Garner's mother." Sometimes my actual name is mentioned as "Gwen Carr, Eric Garner's mother." It took some getting used to, not because I don't want to be mentioned alongside Eric, but it almost became my identity. Before "that day" happened, I was just Gwen Carr. Now it's different.

In print it's even stranger because all of us mothers are identified by our child who has died. I'm always "Gwen Carr (Eric Garner)." That took a little getting used to, but I realized that it was the easiest way to communicate who we were, who I was, but it also meant that I was always reminded of my loss, a perennial parenthetical.

As a mother, that was yet another adjustment I made, another sacrifice I gladly accepted. That is what I have always done and what most mothers do. We give of ourselves for the betterment of others, especially our families. Sometimes it's a thankless job, and sometimes it's filled with grief, but it's the only thing I ever wanted to be. To give birth and watch that child grow to an adult is one of God's blessings, and one that I cherish every day. I always knew that I would be a mother, even from a very young age. It was always part of me. Just like Eric will always be a part of me.

# Chapter 10

―――――――――――――――〇―――――――――――――――

# The Unplanned Activist

If there is no struggle, there is no progress. Those who profess to favor freedom, and deprecate agitation, are men who want crops without plowing up the ground, they want rain without thunder and lightning.

―Frederick Douglass

I DON'T PRETEND TO BE AN expert in the field of activism—actually, just the opposite. I'm still a novice, still learning every day. Each event or speech or TV show is a new experience that helps me learn more about myself and those around me. I just try to do my best with each opportunity. I figure that if I keep getting asked to do more things, then I must be doing something right. My message must be resonating with others; they must be able to relate to my story.

I never planned to become an activist; it just happened. I could have chosen to look the other way, to do something else with my retirement years, but that was not how I wanted to spend my life. I retired from my full-time job, but I didn't retire from life. I still want things to be better for future generations, and for my grandchildren and great-grandchildren. I hope that no other family has to go through what I've been through.

I suppose I could just sit back and live off my pension and have a decent life, maybe move to Florida and soak up the sunshine. That's probably what I would have done had "that day" not happened, or at least that's what I used to say. Instead, I have found myself in some rather incredible situations and met some amazing people, all because I chose not to sit on the sidelines.

I don't think I'm particularly brave or strong, but I am a mother, and trusting my instincts as a parent has served me well. That's what helped me decide to get involved. As a mother, as Eric's mother, I couldn't just watch while other people got involved. How could I do that to Eric and his memory?

This is what I've learned over the past few years.

## BECOMING AN ACTIVIST

- *Find your motivation.* This was the most important and the first piece of the puzzle. You should be getting involved because it's important to you. I learned from being around so many activists that if your heart isn't in it, then it won't work for you.

- *Start slow.* This was important for me because I was still reeling from my son's death—I still am—but I knew that I needed to take things slowly at first and see how it worked out for me. I didn't want to jump in feet first just to quit if things didn't work out. I eased into it, attended some marches, and went from there.

- *Follow the leader.* You might have a lot of ideas about how to implement your ideas, but you should find someone who has been doing it for a while and learn from them. Find out what has worked for them and what hasn't. That doesn't mean that you will do exactly the same, but you can learn from others. If they are passionate about the cause, they will be glad to share what they know with you.

- *There is safety in numbers.* Join an existing group or create one of your own. One of the most impactful ways to create some kind of change is to show that a lot of people feel the same way. That doesn't mean that you can't go it alone. Cynthia and I spent many evenings with just the two of us, but we were glad when others finally started to join.

- *Buckle your seatbelt.* Activism is an unpredictable and often emotional roller coaster full of highs and lows. Actually, it's more like lows and lows, and maybe a high every once in a while. It's tough work and takes time to get into the groove, but if you stick with it, the rewards are worth the effort.

- *Keep your cool.* It's easy to let your emotions take over and react without thinking, but it's important to keep calm. Being an activist can generate negativity from those who don't feel the same way you do. Getting caught up in that can lead to physical confrontations, and that should not be part of your mission. Violence doesn't solve anything.

- *Pass it on.* If you are successful and enjoy getting involved, part of your mission should be educating others and working to bring them aboard with you. Activism is best when it's passed down to others because they have a good understanding of what they're getting into after having watched what you are doing.

- *Trust your instincts.* Any time I've had to make a decision about what to do or even whether to keep going, I stop and take stock, pray, and come to my own conclusion. I can feel when something is right for me. That doesn't mean it's always the best decision, but it does mean that I'm content with my choice. And if that's the case, then I can sleep at night knowing I've done my best.

- *Don't compromise yourself.* This is the most important thing I have learned along the way. People think that if you are an activist, you need to act a certain way. You need to be loud and aggressive and pushy. I can tell you that is not the case. That's initially why I didn't feel like activism was right for me, because that is not my personality. However, I quickly realized that I could use my strengths to get results. Sometimes when you are quieter, people listen even more closely. I felt like my form of compassionate activism worked for me. You have to find what works best for you without changing who you are. Your individuality is the most important thing you can offer. Make it work for you.

Everything I do is to preserve the memory of my sons and to ensure that they are not forgotten. Until the killings stop, I will keep on talking and telling my story as long as people will listen. I realize that I may not always have such a large platform, that folks might get tired of hearing me talk about my loss. If that happens, I will make peace with it because I'll know that I've done all I can.

# A Letter to My Son

I write this letter in memory of you, Eric.

I carried you for nine months, loved you, cherished you, and protected you. Even as an adult, you were still my baby, no matter how old or big you may have been. You were still a respectful, intelligent, and devoted son who grew up to be the family's lawyer and advocate. I miss you greatly.

I still can't believe that you are gone, gone forever; that's just not the way it should be.

Eric, you were supposed to bury me. These tears I cry for you should have been yours weeping for your dearly departed mother. It's just not right. The day you left this earth is one I will never forget. I replay that day in my mind over and over, moment by moment, word for word. It is engraved permanently in my heart; the ache is so deep inside and never goes away.

I hear it mentioned often that "time is supposed to heal your pain," but if I'm being honest, I hope it will remain. I need to feel you constantly just to get through the day. Your life was stolen. That really wasn't fair. They took my firstborn, my future, my heir. If only they had asked if I would take your place, I would have done it willingly, leaving you this world to grace. I pray that you are happy. I pray that you are safe. I pray to God each night to wrap you and keep you in his awesome embrace.

My life without you is empty and dark; the light that once shone has gone out in my heart. Sometimes I hear your laughter. Sometimes I hear you crying out for me and I say, "Oh, God, why wasn't I there for my son?"

Then God answers, "It was not for you to be there that day, Gwen, because they may have had to bury the two of you. Then who would have been left back here to uplift your son Eric's name? Who would be fighting for justice and to change laws for those who will come after him? Who will continue to say his name if you are not here? So I'm leaving you to fight the good fight and be a blessing to others, so now your pain will have a purpose."

So, Eric, I am fighting for justice, although if and when it comes it is no justice for you, but for me it will be closure, knowing I tried to do right by you and all the others, the nameless, the faceless, and all those whom the world doesn't recognize. I still wait for answers. I pray to God for courage and for him to strengthen my faith so I can proceed on this journey. I know I can't go higher until I've been through the fire, so I'm going to take off my shoes and walk on these burning coals. I know God will keep me, as he did the three in the Bible whom they tried to set on fire.

My son, the world knows what you went through; their eyes are open. There is more awareness, more movement because of you. God saw fit for you to become the sacrificial lamb to bring about this uprising. Who would have thought I would have been the vessel that carried you for nine months and everyone in the world would know your name? So, son, I hold this hurt, but it will continue to energize me.

So long for now, but not forever.

Loving you always.

# In Deepest and Loving Memories of My Mom and Dad

A<small>LTHOUGH YOU ARE NOT PHYSICALLY HERE</small> with me, I can feel your presence. I know you are in the midst of all I do. I can hear your voices when I'm in a crowd and more often in the midnight hour when I'm all alone and the wind echoes those sounds I remember as a child.

I can see the legacy you left behind for me to continue. I see in all my surroundings, my children, your children, your grands, my grands, our great-grands, and all the family that you strove to keep together because you said that family is, first and foremost, the most important thing to consider. Mom, oftentimes I remember how good it was to come home and smell the wonderful dishes you were preparing for our dinner. It was no question as to what it would taste like, and if by some chance you had to go on some errand that day, Dad would pick up the slack. You were a good cook too.

I don't remember any hungry days. There was always food, even though we did not have a lot of money. We had stability—we weren't always moving from place to place—thank you for that. You both were my rock. I can't say I love one more than the other because you both were always there. With certain problems I would come to you, Mom, but there were other times I would confide in you, Dad. It was always good to have parents to go to, parents who were always around.

You always reminded my younger sisters and brothers that I was the oldest and they should respect me and listen to what I was saying to them. Although you know your daughter, my sister, Sharon, had a mind of her own and thought things should only be done her way, I loved her dearly anyway. In spite of her ways, I miss her so very much, as I do my brother Joe. I am praying that you are all together embracing one another and sharing the love we all had when we were all here together.

Well, dear Daddy and Mom, I have had quite a full plate these last four years. I know you know by now that I lost Eric in such a brutal and senseless way that it almost took me out. I needed you both to be here with me, as you were when your grandson Emery was murdered. I needed your arms to comfort me. I needed your words of wisdom, Dad. You always knew what to say. I needed you both to lean on, so I would not fall. I needed you, Mom, to take a tissue to wipe my tears. I needed you, Dad, to read the book of Matthew from the Bible, as you always did when I needed a word.

"Where are you two?" I cried. Then the answer came from God up above: "They are with me, my child, as I am with you and have always been there. I am your all, so fear not—even though you cannot see them, their love, compassion, and strength is covering you, and with the goodness, grace, and mercy of my son, Jesus Christ, you will conquer because he is your conqueror. Your parents, they live and love through you."

So now, with that being said, I know that I can continue to fight the good fight. I will continue to do what I know you would be doing with me. I will continue to build on the strong foundation that you left behind. I will continue to pursue justice and try to change laws so Eric's death won't be in vain. Because of parents like you, there are people like me. I would not change a thing about you. I know they say nobody's perfect, but through my eyes you are. I think you were the greatest parents in the universe, and you were mine.

I love you both dearly. You are always going to be in my heart.

# Acknowledgments

FIRST AND FOREMOST, I WANT TO acknowledge my creator, who has enabled me to be and stay strong throughout this challenging journey, who has shown me that all things are possible and how to make a way out of no way.

I would definitely like to thank my family, who was always there steadfastly with me through it all, not just this tragedy but also many other tear-jerking moments.

Thank you to my daughter, Ellisha, who has always wanted to protect and defend me, and whom I love dearly. Thanks also to my sister Marilyn, who always helped me with the kids when they were young, and now I have to help her. That's what family does. Love you, my sister. My brother James, who was a mama's boy and now a sister's boy, love ya. And Marvin, thank you for always checking on big sis and calling me every holiday.

Special thanks to my sister, my friend, Niecie, for always being with me from the beginning of our lives for all the joy, tears, and sorrow. We went through it together and are still standing. Her kids—Damon, Dion, and Desiree—are also awesome.

My thanks to Nadine "Nadia" Fischer, who is my publicist as well as a friend who has guided me on this journey and protected my interests. Thank you for always being concerned about my well-being, my comfort, and my state of mind. You are forever ready to assist whenever you can, and it is my pleasure to have you in my life.

Thank you, Mothers of the Movement—Sybrina, Lucy, Maria, Geneva, and Cleo—for the time we spent together and for the bond we formed. Although we didn't get the results we hoped for, we are not quitters—we are go-getters.

A special thanks to my cousin Mike Garner, president of 100 Black Men and a transit employee who will come to my aid whenever asked with no hesitation, always assuring me that he is only a phone call away.

Thanks to my very special cousin Brenda Hereford, who has been in my life always; thanks for being on my side and by my side whether you thought I was wrong or right. We never had anything but love for each other.

Thank you, Aunt Catherine—at the time I write this, you are ninety-four years old and my only living aunt. I thank you for all the time we have had together (and there is still more to come), your wisdom, your grace, and your spookiness. I know of very, very few ninety-four-year-olds who can still wear five-inch heels, cook, clean, and lay their own carpet. I want to be just like you when I grow up.

Thank you to my niece, Angie, and my cousin, Roslyn, for always being by my side and keeping me informed.

My thanks also go out to Reverend Al Sharpton and the National Action Network (NAN) family for all the support. He has been the one who has been with me from day one after my son Eric was murdered and has continued to keep the fire burning as we look for answers to bring about justice. Even when we bump into a brick wall, the struggle continues.

Thank you, Reverend Daughtry and Mrs. Daughtry, for your many acts of kindness and always being willing to lend a helping hand whenever called upon.

Thank you, Bishop Kareem Evans, for being a family member, friend, and someone I can always call on and depend upon. You will always be in my heart.

Thank you, Bishop Brown, for always reaching out, for caring and sharing, and for being the humble person that you are.

Thanks, Cynthia Davis, for all that you have done and continue to do to try to make this world a better place for us to live, and for your endless devotion.

Thank you, my Christian Love family, who have always loved and supported me. Special thanks to Mother Tea, who always comes to my aid, and all the ministers and members who are always there for me. I will always cherish the late, great, irreplaceable Reverend Ron for supporting my journey. Long live his legacy.

Thank you, Minister Kirsten John Foy, for all you do inside and outside the ministry, for always standing with me and standing up for me at rallies and press conferences, and for just being a friend. You are truly loved by me as well as my family.

Thank you, Pastor Bartley and Lady Bartley, for everything, for being there, for treating us like family, and for your many encouraging words when I need you. You always come through. I love your family, and also your church family.

Thank you, Reverend Shelia Evans-Tranumn, my childhood friend. You have been there for me whenever I call, and even when I don't call on you, you are always ready to help in any way you can.

Thank you, Reverend McColl, for your dedication and strength.

Thank you, Reverend Fletcher and Allisha Fletcher, for your support. You two are awesome.

I want to thank all the ministers, clergy, priests, rabbis, and pastors who reached out after my son's death. Your kindness and warmth made a difference.

Thank you, Ramsey Orta, for bringing about this awareness. Thank you for your courage. Because of the eye of your camera, the world's eyes were opened. You are the most important factor in this movement. Eternally grateful.

Thank you, Hillary, for all you've shown me as a person. Even though you were not elected, you are still my candidate, and I would do it all again if you asked. I appreciate all the lessons learned, all the hard work that went into what you were striving for, and when you lost the election, so did I. Nevertheless, we must push forward.

Thank you, Beyoncé, for reaching out to me and other mothers. I am so grateful to have known you. It was a joy to work with you and be a part of your greatest production, *Lemonade*. Thank you for your strength and personality.

Thank you, Dominique and Ashley Sharpton, for your love and support.

Thank you to all New York mothers and families for working with me, helping me, and always being ready to join in the fight for justice.

Thank you, Justice Committee, Lorda and Yul-San, for all your work and willingness to always support.

Thanks so much, Marion Gray-Hopkins, for always helping to bring the mothers from your area together for this cause.

Thank you, brother-in-law Larry Adams, for all you do for always answering the call and for your readiness to step up to the plate. I don't know what I'd do without you.

Thanks to my longtime friends (golden girls) Herb, Niecie, Gwen, Vi-Mae, Delores Marion, Katie—many things we have been through together, helping when we needed confiding in each other and being there for one another. I appreciate you all.

Thank you, Evelina, my sweet lil' niece, for being who you are. Just stay that way and don't ever change.

Thank you to my niece, Stephanie, for all you do and for just being there if and when I need you.

Thank you, Mandi. You have been there, and I know you will always be there.

Thank you, Wanda and Queen Brown. We make an awesome trio. You ladies know how to hold a sister down.

Thanks to Professor Norma Bowe, her daughter Becca, and the "Be the Change" group for the times they have remembered me and my son in every way and were always willing to help out and do what they could.

Thank you, Samaria, for being so giving of yourself. You are a trooper.

Thanks to all of my North Carolina family, who never fail to call or ask what I need them to do or they would just show up.

Fay, Cookie, Doris, Jimmie Gina, Sharon, Sylvia, Gwen, Sam, and the many others—love every last one of you.

Thank you to my many grandchildren and great-grands, from far and near, for bringing me so much joy. You are the seed of my seed; you will be the ones who succeed in life. So take hold; never give in to negativity; push forward; grace this world with greatness, positivity, and awareness; and add a little more light to your already bright futures.

Thank you, Reverend Johnnie Green, for your wisdom and knowledge and for just being such a down-to-earth human being. It's a pleasure to know you.

Thank you, Kathy Sharpton, for your kindness. Your bright smile lights up a room.

Thank you, Jimmie Gardner, for your continuous support and just being you.

Thanks to my cousin Mat and her daughter, Nekal, for being there for me always.

I want to say thanks to my nieces and nephews, Nettie, Missy, Keisha, Punkin, and Qunicy, for always being respectful and loving.

Thanks to my cousin Jeanie and her children, Tonya, Pamala, Priscilla, Lil Bit, and Troy, for their love, understanding, and always being there for me.

Thanks to my cousins Larry, Estel, and Levonne for always keeping in touch and for caring.

Thank you, Mae Catherine and Ann, just for being you. You are the greatest cousins a person could have.

Thank you, Councilwoman Debbie Rose, for always answering my call and never being too busy to listen.

Thank you, Congresswomen Maxine Waters, for supporting me as well as several other mothers, and for being so caring and comforting.

Thank you, my MTA family, for having my back and being so considerate during my time of grief—all of you guys were great.

Thank you, cousin Valerie, for all your love, for caring, and sharing. Love you so much.

Thank you so much, Congressman Hakeem Jeffries, for your goodness, fairness, and being so easy to talk with. I admire you as a legislator and also as a person.

Thank you, Congresswoman Yvette Clark, for being a friend as well as a go-to person when I needed to get results. You are an awesome human being.

Thank you, Reverend Curtis, for your pleasant and humble demeanor, for always being ready to listen and knowing just the right thing to say.

Thanks to Eugene Lucas and his wife, Robin, who live in Los Angeles. You always open your home to me when I'm in town. I grew up on the same street as Eugene's father, and they treat me like family.

Thank you, LaDavia. You are one of the sweetest people I know, always ready and willing to help no matter what the circumstance.

Thank you, Tish James, for your support.

Thank you, Detective Rios, you have been a blessing in my life and one of the nicest people I know.

Thank you, Gov. A. Cuomo, for publicly acknowledging me and all the New York families who worked to get the executive order for the special prosecutor that is now an important piece that may soon be law.

Thank you to my cousin Lolly and his wife Sharon for being the people they are and the parents they are.

My niece, Stephanie Skinner, who is always here to do whatever it takes to get me through whatever it is.

My niece, Kim, I always loved you and cared about your well-being.

My niece, Lil Ma, you are my most strong-minded and opinionated niece, and I love you for that.

Brooklyn borough president Eric Adams, thank you for your support in helping me fight for a great cause.

Council members Charles and Inez Barron, thanks for always being there when called upon.

Thank you, Mr. Mickens, for always checking on me.

Thank you, Reverend Curtis, for caring and your wonderful words of encouragement.

Thank you, Mrs. Louise Gallman, for being there through the years. You are my mom and dad's oldest friend, and I love you very much.

Thank you, Rachael Noerdlinger, for being a friend and a person with such courageous strength.

To my Florida family—Cynthia, all her children, Greg's children, Curtis, Lorenzo, and their children—thank you all for always sharing and showing me so much love.

I want to say thank you to the late, great Melvin Cauley and to his wife, Sol. Until his death a year ago, he was always checking to see if I was OK. We have been friends since we were kids. I miss you, Melvin.

Thanks, Kim Nesbitt, funeral director in Elizabeth, New Jersey, for helping and supporting me since I've known you. You are a very giving person.

Thank you, Councilman Robert Cornegy Jr., for being there for me and my family and for always answering the call.

Thanks to Lenny Green and his sidekick, Donna Hayes, for their concern and kindness.

Thank you, Jumaane Williams, for always standing up for what is right and with me.

Also, thanks to Felicia D. Henderson and Sara Finney, writer and creator of *The Quad*.

Special thank you to my literary agent, Diane Nine, and to Jon Sisk at Rowman & Littlefield for helping me through this process.

Finally, thank you to my collaborator, Dave Smitherman, who helped me tell my story.

For anyone I haven't thanked individually, I thank you all; you've been a blessing in my life.

# Index

191

# About the Author

As the matriarch of one of Staten Island's largest African American families, **Gwen Carr** has earned nationwide recognition as the mother of the late Eric Garner, who was murdered by New York police in July 2014. Because the incident was captured on a cell phone video and posted online, his death has played an integral part in raising awareness about the issue of police brutality in the United States, particularly for the Black community.

Gwen Carr's story began in South Brooklyn, where she lived most of her life and raised her family. A longtime employee of both the United States Postal Service and New York City's Metropolitan Transportation Authority, she had planned to retire before the tragedy occurred. Now Mrs. Carr has become an activist, determined to hold the city accountable for the shocking treatment of her son. With three children, fifteen grandchildren, and six great-grandchildren, she represents the voice of several generations, all of whom have suffered greatly from the loss of their beloved Eric.

To assist with the healing of others, the nonprofit organization the Garner Way Foundation was established. Within the foundation, Mrs. Carr facilitates the program This Stops Today, which provides ongoing support and education to the ever-increasing victims of violence and to the families suffering from tragedy and loss. The name of the program comes from her own son's words. Immediately before his death, Eric Garner said to the police, "This stops today," to express his frustration with their constant profiling and harassment.

As the legal proceedings continue in the case of her son, Gwen Carr's maternal sensibilities will not allow a moment's pause in the fight for justice, and she will forever remain stridently dedicated to the cause. Learn more about her mission at www.ThisStopsToday .com.